Joe's
30-Minute
Meals

Joe's 30-Minute Meals

100 QUICK AND HEALTHY RECIPES

JOE WICKS
The Body Coach

bluebird
books for life

CONTENTS

Joe's 30-Minute Meals

Thanks so much for deciding to pick up this book. I'm really excited to be sharing my favourite 30-minute recipes with you. My aim with this – as with all of my books – is to inspire you to cook simple, quick and healthy recipes that will help you to feel great.

Ever since I learned to cook healthy food and realized what a massive difference fuelling myself with fresh, home-cooked food made to my energy levels and mood, I've wanted to get as many people as possible cooking.

Nothing makes me happier than meeting people who have never really enjoyed cooking before or have no confidence in the kitchen but are now enjoying cooking using my recipes. I met a husband who said he hadn't cooked once for his wife until he picked up my book and now cooks a recipe every night of the week for her. I believe there's no greater feeling than getting confident in the kitchen and learning how to make healthy, tasty food at home for yourself, partner or kids.

When I started creating recipe books, I focused on speed. Who doesn't want a 15-minute meal they can whip up straight after work when they are absolutely starving? I wanted to stop people just going for the easy option – the greasy takeaway or kebab – and realize they could make something that tastes way better in the same amount of time.

Sometimes, 15 minutes just isn't enough time as it means the cooking methods are a bit limiting. With this book, I'm still about speed and keeping prep time down to a minimum. After all, half an hour isn't much – especially if we've planned ahead and prepped like a boss. And I don't know about you, but once I start getting stuck in to the kitchen, I find it really fun.

To sustain long-term success, it's really important to keep your diet varied and your flavours interesting. That's what *Joe's 30-Minute Meals* sets out to do. Some of the recipes you just assemble super quickly and bung in the oven, then you can chill out with your partner or family or even better sneak in a cheeky workout. Some of the recipes like Dukkah-spiced Chicken (see page 93) are a little more work, but totally worth it on the flavour front.

ANYBODY CAN DO IT

When I started to try to create healthy meals, I didn't even know how to cook an egg properly or which flavours go well together.

But once I got going, there was no stopping me. It's amazing how much you can learn when it comes to cooking techniques and understanding flavours. This book is going to give you the confidence you need to whip up delicious food so you never have to go back to the ready meals and takeaways that don't do anything for your long-term health or happiness.

And you don't need to be a trained cook. My recipes are simple and straightforward with some shortcuts. It's all about putting good flavours together – and that's not hard.

Some people tell me they think they can't do this because they have never cooked or they don't come from a family where everyone sat around the table over delicious home-cooked food. I didn't. And if I can learn to cook – and even write six cookbooks – anybody can do it. It's just about doing a little planning and making a start and the recipes in this book will be the perfect starting point.

CHAPTERS IN THIS BOOK

I've organized this book by main ingredients: All-Day Breakfast, Chicken, Beef and Pork and so on. I hope this makes it easy for you to find the recipes you want really fast. I genuinely think there is something for everyone in this book with a real variety ranging

from easy Asian stir-fries and curries to tasty Italian pastas and risottos. Be sure to give my Sausage & Mushroom Pie a go if you loved the pies in my previous books (see page 177).

I've also added some sweet treats because everyone deserves a treat now and again. And some of these treats are still pretty healthy like my Baked Maple Apples and Blackcurrant Poached Pears (see pages 219 and 220).

PART OF A HEALTHY LIFESTYLE

Although there's no exercise in this book, any of you who know me will know that for me, good food is just one part of living a healthy lifestyle. The other big factor is being active.

My philosophy around food and fitness is really the same thing: it's all in your hands. You can create the kind of life you want – even if it feels daunting and you have never done any exercise before or cooked anything from scratch. It's never too late to start living the life you really want to live – and when that looks like eating Teriyaki Ginger Chicken (yes please) or Swedish-style Meatballs, you'll find yourself so motivated you won't even believe it. None of this is complicated.

In this book you'll find recipes that are perfect for a lazier day when you're not getting up to much activity (hopefully just a couple of days a week!). I've labelled those reduced-carb. Other recipes are to replenish your energy when you've done a workout. Those are labelled carb-refuel dishes. It's important to keep it balanced and varied.

My advice is to do four or five quick workouts a week. And when I say quick, I really mean it. They often come in at under 20 minutes. I'm a fan of High Intensity Interval Training (HIIT for short) and you can find hundreds of my free workouts on my Youtube channel – TheBodycoachTV. You can do them in your front room or the park – you don't even need any equipment. And the more energy you burn, the more you can tuck in to my carb-rich favourites like Chicken Fried Rice (see page 44) and my Tandoori Cod Burgers (see page 110).

ENJOYING LIFE

Feeling energized and fuelling your body with healthy nutrient-rich food is important. But I don't want you to feel like this is just another thing you 'have' to do – like a New Year Resolution or a 30-day programme. I do this because it makes me feel great. And I really believe you're going to feel great and have more energy and fun if you treat yourself to the delicious food in this book.

Today there's more talk about mental health than ever before. The way I look at it, we have to begin at the basics. What are we eating? Are we moving enough? Exercise is one of the biggest stress-busters around. And we all know the low mood that can come from overdoing it on the sugar front or eating junk food and relying on caffeine for energy. The recipes in this book are going to fuel your body and give you energy all day long.

I'm passionate about making sure I can do my part to help people find easy ways to work healthy habits into their lives. And I love to do that with my workouts, with a free schools HIIT programme and of course most of all with my recipes. What I'm about is fun and feeling good. And I know from my own life – and the tens of thousands of people I've now worked with – that eating generous portions of incredible food and maintaining a healthy exercise regime (without overdoing the hours in the gym so there's no time for living) is the secret to a happier life.

I hope you enjoy my new recipes and the energy they give you.

LOVE,

Joe Wicks

STAY IN TOUCH

🐦 📘 👻 📷 @thebodycoach
▶️ The Body Coach TV

Stocking up

I'm always banging on about the importance of meal preparation – I call it 'prepping like a boss'! And one thing that really makes it easy to cook healthy and tasty food, is stocking up on key ingredients so you have them to hand when you need them. Then you can just pick up some chicken or sea bass or something on the way home from work and you're good to go.

I've put my favourite standby ingredients down here. Most of them are ordinary things you'll use again and again. A few are a bit more like treats, and they can seem pricey, but when you add up what you're likely to save on take-aways, ready meals and frozen pizza, you'll see that you're winning on cost as well as creating much healthier, better-tasting grub.

FRESH & FROZEN

Basics

- Tortilla wraps
- Garlic
- Ginger
- Onions (such as white, red, spring, shallots)
- Eggs
- Greek yoghurt

- Basic cheese (such as mature cheddar, goat's cheese, parmesan, mozzarella, feta)
- Avocado
- Fresh greens (such as kale, spinach, pak choy, watercress, brussels sprouts, cabbage)

- Midget trees
- Salad greens (such as lettuce, rocket, cucumber, radishes)
- Mushrooms
- Sweet potatoes
- Aubergines
- Frozen peas
- Frozen spinach

Extras I love

- Olives
- Edamame beans
- Fresh herbs

- Special cheese (such as taleggio, manchego, burrata, gruyère)
- Chilli peppers

- Lemongrass stalks
- Fresh lemons and limes
- Pomegranate seeds

STORE-CUPBOARD

Basics

- Porridge oats
- Rice (such as pre-cooked, arborio or otherwise)
- Pre-cooked puy lentils and quinoa
- Pasta (such as fusilli, shells, orzo, fresh noodles, dried noodles)
- Tinned beans and pulses (kidney beans, black beans, cannellini beans, chickpeas)
- Quick-cook polenta

- Filo pastry
- Nuts and seeds (such as almonds, walnuts, pine nuts, cashews, pecan nuts, sesame seeds, nigella seeds)
- Tomato puree
- Chopped tomatoes and passata
- Coconut oil
- Olive oil
- Stock (chicken, vegetable, fish)

- Sea salt and black pepper
- Basic spices (such as dried chilli flakes; garam masala; ground turmeric; cayenne pepper; smoked paprika; ground cinnamon, ground cumin; ground coriander)
- Light soy sauce
- Red and white wine vinegar
- Dijon mustard
- Jarred roasted red peppers
- Jarred sundried tomatoes

Extras I love

- Tahini
- Sriracha
- Fish sauce
- Sesame oil
- Miso powder or paste
- Jarred anchovies

- Jarred capers
- Ready-made pastes (such as harissa, chipotle and tikka masala curry)
- Balsamic vinegar
- Rice vinegar

- Special spices (such as star anise; mustard seeds; cardamom pods; fennel seeds; fenugreek seeds; Sichuan peppercorns; dukkah mix; sumac; saffron)

All-day
Breakfast

Smashed peas

HAM & EGG MUFFINS

* Serves 2

1 chicken stock cube
300g frozen peas
2 English muffins, cut in half
4 eggs
1 red chilli, finely chopped
3 spring onions, trimmed and finely sliced
1 tbsp coriander, chopped
juice of ½ lime
salt and black pepper
4 thick slices of thick-cut, deli-style ham, visible fat removed

Bring two pans of water to the boil and add the chicken stock cube to one of them. When the stock pan is boiling, drop the frozen peas into the stock and boil for about 8 minutes or until the peas are very tender. Before you drain the peas, scoop out half a mugful of the cooking liquid and keep to one side.

Drain the peas and put your muffins on to toast. Carefully crack your eggs into the hot water, reducing the heat until the water is just 'burping'. Cook the eggs for about 4 minutes for a runny yolk, then carefully lift them out with a slotted spoon and drain on kitchen roll.

Tip the peas back into the pan they were cooked in and add the red chilli, sliced spring onions, coriander and lime juice, along with a splash of the reserved stock and a good pinch of both salt and pepper. Use a hand blender to blitz the peas into a coarse-textured mix – I like it to be smooth in parts, but also quite coarse. Add a little more stock if necessary.

Plate up the hot, toasted muffins and top each one with a slice of ham, a mound of the peas and a perfectly poached egg.

CHEESE, SPINACH & HAM
everyday omelette

* Serves 1

3 eggs
salt and black pepper
knob of butter
large handful of baby
spinach leaves
20g cheddar, grated
75g good-quality ham,
roughly torn
green salad, to serve

Crack the eggs into a bowl and add a tiny sprinkle of salt and a good grind of pepper. Beat the eggs together with a fork.

Heat the butter over a medium to high heat in a small non-stick frying pan. When the butter is bubbling and melted, drop in the spinach and stir to wilt.

As soon as all of the spinach has just wilted, pour in the beaten eggs.

Using a wooden spoon, beat the eggs around the pan as if you are scrambling them. Continue to do this until the mixture starts to resemble very loose scrambled egg. At this point, reduce the heat to low and spread the egg out over the base of the pan.

Sprinkle the cheese over half of the omelette and place the ham on top of the cheese. Turn off the heat.

Give the omelette a poke around the edges to ensure it's set, then, lifting it up by the handle, gently tip the pan away from you and, using your spoon, lift the edge closest to you and roll it over.

Pull out your plate, then tip the omelette onto the plate so that the browned bottom of the omelette becomes the top.

Serve up your classic omelette with a little side salad.

CHOCOLATE MALT
overnight oats

* Serves 4
* Make ahead

55g fat-free Greek yoghurt
3 scoops (90g) chocolate
protein powder
1 scoop (30g) low-sugar
malted-milk drink powder
600ml almond milk
275g porridge oats

To serve
handful of raspberries
handful of roasted hazelnuts,
chopped

Whisk together the yoghurt, protein powder, malted-milk drink powder and almond milk until there are no lumps.

Stir in the porridge oats and leave in a container overnight.

Serve with the raspberries and chopped hazelnuts.

Photo overleaf

GOAT'S CHEESE & CHORIZO
morning muffins

* Makes 12
* Make ahead

2 tsp coconut oil
125g cooking chorizo, cut into
5mm pieces
100g frozen peas
75g soft goat's cheese
8 eggs
salt and black pepper
125g jarred roasted red
peppers, drained and cut
into thin 3cm strips
4 spring onions, trimmed and
finely sliced

Preheat the oven to 190°C (fan 170°C/gas mark 5).

Heat the oil in a small frying pan over a medium heat and add the chorizo pieces. Fry for 3–4 minutes until cooked through, then turn off the heat and leave.

Bring a kettle to the boil. Tip the peas into a bowl, pour the boiling water over the peas and leave to sit for 1 minute. Drain and leave to one side.

Tip the goat's cheese into a bowl and crack in 2 eggs along with a pinch of salt and pepper. Whisk the cheese together with the eggs until fully combined. Whisk in the remaining eggs, then stir in the cooked chorizo along with any of the red cooking oil, the peas, red peppers and spring onions. Mix well.

Equally divide the mixture between the twelve holes of a muffin tin, then slide into the oven and bake for 15 minutes. When cooked, remove and leave to cool.

Masala eggy bread
WITH QUICK TOMATO RELISH

* Serves 2

6 eggs

2 tsp garam masala

2 tsp ground turmeric

½ tsp cayenne pepper

salt and black pepper

4 medium slices of bread

1 tbsp coconut oil

½ tsp brown mustard seeds

2 cloves garlic, finely chopped

½ red onion, peeled and finely diced

3cm ginger, peeled and finely chopped

1 green chilli, finely sliced

½ tsp ground cumin

½ tsp ground coriander

2 large ripe tomatoes, roughly chopped into chunks

handful of fresh coriander, chopped, to serve

Whisk together the eggs with the garam masala, turmeric and cayenne pepper and a good pinch of both salt and pepper. Pour the mix into a baking dish, or something deep and wide. Lay the bread slices in the mix and turn them over a few times to start them soaking well.

Soak the bread for 5–10 minutes, turning every now and again.

Meanwhile, make the relish. Melt half of the oil in a saucepan over a medium to high heat, then add the mustard seeds. Fry for 30 seconds, then add the garlic, onion, ginger and green chilli and fry, stirring regularly, for 4 minutes.

Sprinkle in the cumin and coriander and stir to combine. Slide in the tomatoes and turn the heat down a little (if your tomatoes aren't very ripe, add a splash of water). Cook the relish for 10 minutes, stirring every now and again.

It is likely you will have to cook the eggy bread in two batches. So melt half of the remaining oil in a large non-stick frying pan over a medium to high heat, then cook the bread gently for about 2 minutes on each side. It should be golden brown on the outside and cooked all the way through. Transfer the bread to a piece of kitchen roll to blot off excess oil, then wipe out the pan and repeat the process with the remaining oil and soaked bread.

Serve up the eggy bread with the relish and a sprinkling of chopped coriander.

Cover the leftover relish and keep it in the fridge for up to 5 days.

Baked eggs
IN HERBY MUSHROOMS

*Serves 4

8 portobello mushrooms
40ml olive oil
2 cloves garlic, minced
4 sprigs of thyme, leaves only
salt and black pepper
4 big handfuls of baby
spinach leaves
8 eggs
4 tbsp grated parmesan
600g thick-cut, deli-style ham,
to serve

Preheat the oven to 200°C (fan 180°C/gas mark 6).

Take each mushroom one at a time, upturn it and break off the stalk. Using a spoon, scoop out all the brown gills to leave yourself hollowed mushrooms. Line them up, hollowed-out side up, on a flat baking tray.

Mix together the olive oil, garlic and thyme along with a pinch of salt and pepper. Drizzle the garlic and herb mix over the scooped-out side of the mushrooms, then slide the tray into the oven and bake for 10 minutes.

While the mushrooms are baking, tip the spinach into a sieve and bring a full kettle to the boil. When boiled, pour the water over the waiting spinach to wilt it, then immediately cool it with cold running water. Pick up the spinach with both hands and give it a big squeeze to remove as much of the liquid as you can.

After 10 minutes, remove the mushrooms from the oven and lightly rub them with kitchen roll to absorb any liquid that may have been produced.

Give the spinach one last squeeze, then divide it among the eight mushrooms, creating a sort of ring within the scooped-out circle.

Crack an egg into the centre of each spinach-lined mushroom and sprinkle the parmesan over the top. Slide the mushrooms back into the oven and bake for 12 minutes.

While the eggs are baking, heat the ham by placing it on a plate and pouring over a little hot water. Cover it with cling film and zap it in the microwave.

After 12 minutes, the yolks should be just runny. Serve the mushrooms straight up with the warmed ham.

Carrot fritters

WITH EGGS & HALLOUMI

* Serves 2
(makes 4)
* Make ahead
* Freeze ahead

1 small carrot, peeled and grated (about 110g)

¼ courgette, trimmed and grated (about 60g)

2 spring onions, trimmed and finely sliced

30g ground almonds

10g plain flour

3 eggs

salt and black pepper

½ tbsp coconut oil

6 slices of halloumi

sweet chilli sauce, to serve

Mix together the grated carrot and courgette in a bowl along with the sliced spring onions, ground almonds, flour and one of the eggs. Season with a little salt and pepper and then stir everything well with a fork to bring it together. The mixture can appear to be a bit wet – don't be tempted to add extra flour.

Put a pan of water on to boil for your poached eggs.

Melt half of the coconut oil in a large non-stick frying pan over a medium to high heat, then spoon the mixture in, making four roughly equal-sized circles. If you don't have a large enough pan to fry all four at the same time, then fry them in batches.

Fry the fritters for 2–3 minutes on each side, or until they are browned and the egg is cooked all the way through. Transfer the fritters to a piece of kitchen roll to dab off any excess oil.

Carefully crack the remaining eggs into the hot water, reducing the heat until the water is just 'burping'. Cook the eggs for about 4 minutes for a runny yolk, then carefully lift them out with a slotted spoon and drain on kitchen roll.

While the eggs are poaching, wipe out the pan and add the remaining oil. Melt the coconut oil over a medium to high heat, then add the halloumi and fry for about 45 seconds on each side, or until nicely browned and soft in the middle.

Serve up the fritters, laying the halloumi on top, then finish with a poached egg and sweet chilli sauce.

Full English bake-up

* Serves 4

1 tbsp sunflower oil
8 good-quality sausages
or chipolatas
8 rashers of smoked
streaky bacon
2 tomatoes, cut in half
6 large chestnut mushrooms,
roughly halved
4 sprigs of thyme, leaves only
4 eggs

To serve
4 large handfuls of
spinach leaves
brown sauce

Preheat the oven to 210°C (fan 190°C/gas mark 6–7).

Pour the oil onto a flat baking tray and slide into the oven to preheat for 5 minutes. Remove the tray and quickly lay the sausages on, then slide the tray back into the oven and cook for 10 minutes (or 5 minutes if you're using chipolatas).

Slide the tray out of the oven, quickly flip the sausages and then lay the bacon rashers on and around the sausages before sliding the tray back into the oven and cooking for a further 5 minutes.

Remove the tray again and dot around the tomatoes and mushrooms. Sprinkle with the thyme leaves, then slide the tray back into the oven and cook for 10 minutes.

Carefully remove the tray and pour off any excess liquid released by the mushrooms.

Push the cooking ingredients around a little to create four small wells in the mixture. Crack the eggs into the small wells, then slide the tray back into the oven for a final 5 minutes.

Serve with a handful of spinach and some brown sauce.

* This only works with decent-quality ingredients.
  Cheap bacon will flood your tray with water and give
  you a 'full poach-up'!

Tahini & yoghurt eggs
WITH CHORIZO

* Serves 2

240g Greek yoghurt
60g tahini
1 fat clove garlic, minced
175g cooking chorizo, cut into
5mm pieces
4 eggs
½ bunch of parsley, roughly
chopped

MAKE IT VEG
Simply drop the chorizo
and add a handful of
pine nuts.

Pour about 5cm of water into a medium pan and bring to the boil. Put another larger pan almost filled to the brim with water on to heat as well – this will be for poaching the eggs.

Tip the yoghurt and tahini into a bowl that sits snugly on top of the medium pan, making sure the base of the bowl does not touch the boiling water. Add the garlic and a little splash of water to loosen the ingredients, then sit the bowl over the steaming pan of water. Leave the ingredients to warm through, stirring every now and again for about 5 minutes, or until just warmed through.

Tip the chorizo pieces into a small non-stick frying pan over a medium heat. As the chorizo warms, it releases oil. Let it fry in this oil until lightly browned and crisp, then take the pan off the heat.

Carefully crack your eggs into the hot water, reducing the heat until the water is just 'burping'. Cook the eggs for about 4 minutes for a runny yolk, then carefully lift them out with a slotted spoon and drain on kitchen roll.

When ready to plate up, give the tahini sauce a stir – it is likely you will have to add a little more warm water to loosen the sauce to the consistency of very thick double cream.

Divide the sauce into two shallow bowls, scoop the eggs onto the sauce, then top with the fried chorizo pieces, drizzling over some of the delicious oil.

Finish with a good covering of chopped parsley and get stuck in.

Chicken

Mexican tortilla
WITH CHICKEN & FETA

* Serves 2
* Make ahead

2 tbsp coconut oil

1 x 250g skinless chicken breast, chopped

2 red onions, peeled and thinly sliced

6 eggs

salt and black pepper

2 large fistfuls of spinach

80g feta

50g tinned sweetcorn, drained

1 avocado, de-stoned and cut into thin wedges

small bunch of coriander, roughly chopped

1 red chilli, finely sliced – remove the seeds if you don't like it hot

Melt half of the coconut oil in a medium non-stick ovenproof frying pan. Slide in the chicken pieces and stir-fry gently for 7 minutes until the chicken is cooked. Check by slicing into it to make sure the meat is white all the way through, with no raw pink bits left. Leave to one side.

Melt the remaining oil in the pan over a medium to high heat. Add the sliced onions and cook for 10 minutes, stirring every now and again until the onions are soft and lightly browned.

Turn on your grill to maximum.

Crack the eggs into a bowl and beat together with a small pinch of salt and pepper. Crank up the heat under the onions to maximum and add the spinach, turning it regularly until wilted.

Pour the beaten eggs into the pan, and as the tortilla sets round the edges, draw the cooked egg into the middle, allowing the centre to be filled with raw egg. Continue to cook your eggs like this until the mix is three-quarters cooked through. Turn the heat off under the pan and crumble the feta evenly over the surface of the egg.

Slide the frying pan under the hot grill. Let the tortilla grill for 2–3 minutes, or until the feta is just starting to brown and there is no raw egg visible on the surface of the tortilla.

Remove the pan from the grill, carefully slide the tortilla onto a chopping board and scatter with the sweetcorn, cooked chicken, avocado, coriander and red chilli. Wedge it up and serve.

Teriyaki ginger chicken
WITH AUBERGINE & RICE

* Serves 4

1 tbsp coconut oil

4 cloves garlic, finely chopped

1 large aubergine, trimmed and cut into 4cm batons (275g)

100ml water

35ml light soy sauce

2cm ginger, peeled and roughly cut into small pieces

1 x 300g chicken breast, cut into 1cm strips

125g oyster mushrooms, large ones, torn in half

600g pre-cooked rice

3 spring onions, trimmed and finely sliced

Melt half of the coconut oil in a saucepan over a medium to high heat, then add the garlic and fry for 30 seconds. Throw in the aubergine on top. Fry the aubergine and garlic together for about 2 minutes, then add the water and soy sauce. Bring the liquid to the boil, cover with a lid and simmer on a low heat for 15 minutes, or until the aubergine pieces have pretty much broken down. Keep half an eye on the water levels – add little splashes of water to the pan if you think it's necessary.

While the aubergine is cooking, heat up the remaining oil in a large frying pan or wok over a high heat, then add the ginger and sliced chicken breast and stir-fry for 2 minutes. Add the mushrooms and continue to stir-fry for 2–3 minutes or until you are happy the chicken is fully cooked through and the mushrooms are just starting to wilt a little.

Heat up your rice in the microwave.

Serve up mounds of rice topped with the tasty aubergine and chicken and sprinkled with the sliced spring onions.

* I like using pre-cooked rice, but if you prefer you could cook 200g rice according to packet instructions.

Grilled lemon chicken
WITH CAULIFLOWER RICE

* Serves 4
* Make ahead

4 x 200g skinless chicken breasts

3 tsp fresh oregano leaves, roughly chopped

3 tsp fresh thyme leaves, roughly chopped

juice of 1 lemon

4 tbsp olive oil

800g cauliflower florets (2 caulis)

5 spring onions, trimmed and finely sliced

1 tsp sweet smoked paprika

½ tsp ground cumin

salt and black pepper

watercress, to serve

Take each chicken breast one at a time and lay lengthways on your chopping board. Cut into the side of the breast as if you were trying to cut the breast in half horizontally, but stop about 1cm from slicing all the way through. Open the meat up like a book and give it a little push with the palm of your hand to flatten. Place in a large tray and repeat the process with the remaining chicken.

Sprinkle in the oregano and thyme leaves and add the lemon juice and 3 tablespoons of the olive oil. Leave the chicken to sit for 5 minutes.

While the chicken is marinating, blitz up the cauliflower florets until they resemble couscous.

When you are ready to eat, heat up both a griddle pan and a large frying pan over a high heat. When the griddle pan is hot, drain the excess oil from the chicken breasts and griddle on each side for 3 minutes, by which time they should be fully cooked through and nicely browned. Check by slicing into the chicken to make sure the meat is white all the way through, with no raw pink bits left.

In the large frying pan, heat up the remaining olive oil and when it is hot, add the spring onions and fry for 30 seconds, then add the cauliflower and cook, stirring regularly over the high heat for 5 minutes. Sprinkle in the ground spices along with a generous pinch of salt and pepper, then take off the heat.

Serve up the cauliflower topped with the chicken, and finally add a good handful of watercress per person.

Chicken fried rice

WITH MANGO & BASIL

* Serves 2

½ tbsp coconut oil

4 spring onions, trimmed and finely sliced

2 cloves garlic, finely chopped

1 x 300g skinless chicken breast, cut into 1cm slices

1 small carrot, peeled and diced

5 baby sweetcorn, cut in half lengthways

80g frozen peas

400g pre-cooked rice

1½ tbsp soy sauce

1 tsp sesame oil

1 mango, peeled and cut into rough 2cm cubes

2 red chillies, finely sliced – remove the seeds if you don't like the heat

small bunch of basil, roughly chopped

Melt the coconut oil in a large frying pan or wok over a high heat, then chuck in the spring onions and garlic and fry for 30 seconds. Add the chicken slices and stir-fry for 2 minutes, then add the carrot, sweetcorn and frozen peas. Stir-fry everything together for 3 minutes, by which time the chicken should be just about cooked through.

Add the rice and toss together with the other ingredients. Add a splash of water to the pan, and let it steam up to help separate and warm through the rice and finish off cooking the chicken and vegetables. Fry the rice until you are happy the rice is completely heated through.

Take the mix off the heat and stir through the soy sauce and sesame oil, then, when the sauces are well combined, stir in the mango pieces.

Serve up the rice, topped with the fiery chilli slices and chopped basil.

* I like using pre-cooked rice, but if you prefer you could cook 135g rice according to packet instructions and allow to cool before adding to the pan.

Chicken & aubergine 'pizza'

* Serves 2
* Make ahead

2 aubergines
3–4 tbsp olive oil
10g tomato puree
200g chopped tomatoes
1 clove garlic, roughly chopped
½ tsp dried oregano
salt and black pepper
2 x 180g skinless chicken breasts
100g taleggio or mozzarella
rocket, to serve

MAKE IT VEG
Omit the chicken and give the pizza a generous sprinkling of pumpkin seeds, sunflower seeds, cashews or pistachios.

Preheat the oven to 200°C (fan 180°C/gas mark 6).

Cut each aubergine lengthways into 8–10 slices, roughly 5mm thick (doesn't need to be an exact science!).

Heat a large griddle pan over a high heat and drizzle the aubergine slices with a little olive oil. Griddle the aubergine slices in batches, cooking them for about 1 minute on each side – they should be nicely marked by the pan and just cooked through.

While the aubergine slices are cooking, slide the tomato puree, chopped tomatoes, garlic clove and dried oregano into a food processor and blitz until smooth. Season with a little salt and pepper.

Put each chicken breast between two pieces of cling film, and using a rolling pin, lightly beat until slightly thinned to an even thickness. Brush each side with olive oil and cook on the hot griddle pan for 6–8 minutes on each side, until cooked through. Check by slicing into the chicken to make sure the meat is white all the way through, with no raw pink bits left.

Build your pizza by creating a circle, about 20cm in diameter, with some of the aubergine slices, then cover the middle with a few more. Spread over about a third of the tomato sauce, then lay the remaining aubergine slices on top, overlapping them to create a roughly even circle.

Spoon the remaining tomato sauce over the top, lay the cooked chicken on and then dot with taleggio. Bake the 'pizza' in the oven for 10 minutes.

Remove the 'pizza' from the oven, top with rocket and cut into wedges.

Photo overleaf

I love taleggio, so it takes pride of place on top of this pizza, but any cheese – from mozzarella to a blue cheese – would work well. If you decide to make this ahead, simply build your pizza, then leave in the fridge until ready to cook.

JOE'S BANGIN'

chicken balti

* Serves 4
* Make ahead
* Freeze ahead

1½ tbsp coconut oil

2 red onions, peeled and cut into chunks

5 cardamom pods, bruised with the side of a knife

1 stick of cinnamon

4cm ginger, peeled and minced

5 cloves garlic, minced

1 large green chilli, slit down the length

1 red pepper, de-seeded and cut into 3cm chunks

1 green pepper, de-seeded and cut into 3cm chunks

1 tsp ground turmeric

2 tsp garam masala

18 cherry tomatoes, cut in half

150ml water

3 x 200g skinless chicken breasts, cut into large chunks

bunch of coriander, roughly chopped

700g pre-cooked rice

Melt the coconut oil in a large casserole dish over a medium to high heat. Blitz the onions in a food processor until they're pretty much a puree, then tip into the hot, melted oil along with the cardamom pods and the cinnamon stick. Cook for 12 minutes, stirring regularly.

Add the ginger and garlic and cook for a further 2 minutes, then add the chilli, red pepper, green pepper, turmeric and garam masala and cook, stirring regularly, for 2 more minutes.

Crank up the heat a little and chuck in the cherry tomatoes and the water. Bring to the boil, then add the chicken pieces. Simmer the curry for 10 minutes, or until you are sure the chicken is fully cooked through. Check by slicing into one of the larger pieces to make sure the meat is white all the way through, with no raw pink bits left.

Finish the curry with the chopped coriander, and serve with steaming-hot rice.

Do not reduce the onion cooking time because it's pretty much the most important part of cooking. I like using pre-cooked rice, but if you prefer you could cook 235g rice according to packet instructions.

Paprika & lentil stew

WITH HONEY-GLAZED CHICKEN

* Serves 4

1 tbsp coconut oil

1 large onion, peeled and diced

2 sticks of celery, trimmed and diced

100g kale, thick stalks removed

1 fresh bay leaf

1 large fennel bulb, trimmed and diced

3 tomatoes, roughly chopped into 2cm chunks

1½ tsp sweet smoked paprika

275g pre-cooked puy lentils

200ml chicken stock

salt and black pepper

4 x 180–200g chicken breasts

2 stalks of rosemary, needles only, finely chopped

4 tsp honey

Melt half of the coconut oil in a large high-sided frying pan over a medium to high heat, then add the onion. Fry, stirring regularly for about 8 minutes, or until the onions have softened and taken on a little colour.

Add the celery, kale, bay leaf and fennel and continue to fry, stirring every now and again for 4 minutes, then crank up the heat and add the tomatoes, paprika, lentils and stock, along with a good pinch of both salt and pepper. Bring the liquid to the boil, then reduce to a simmer and cook for 10 minutes.

While the stew is cooking, take each breast one at a time and slice into the side, cutting almost all the way through but not quite. Open the breast up like a book and push it with the palm of your hand to flatten it slightly. Repeat the process with the remaining breasts.

Melt the remaining oil in a large non-stick frying pan over a medium to high heat. Season the breasts all over with salt and pepper and sprinkle with the chopped rosemary. When the oil is melted and hot, carefully lay the meat in the hot pan and fry for 4 minutes on one side, then flip and cook for a further 3 minutes, by which time the chicken should be cooked all the way through. Check by slicing into the chicken to make sure the meat is white all the way through, with no raw pink bits left.

Turn the heat off under the pan and pour the honey over the cooked breasts, turning them in the honey to glaze.

Serve the chicken on top of a steaming bowl of the stew.

SINGAPORE
chicken udon noodles

* Serves 2

½ tbsp coconut oil

3 cloves garlic, roughly chopped

2 lemongrass stalks, tender white part only, finely sliced

1 star anise

2 bird's eye chillies, slit lengthways – remove the seeds if you don't like it hot

4cm ginger, peeled and finely chopped

small bunch of coriander, stalks only

6 spring onions, trimmed and finely sliced

2 x 200g skinless chicken breasts, cut into 1cm strips

6 baby sweetcorn, sliced in half

120g mange tout or green beans

400g ready-to-eat udon noodles

1 tbsp mild curry powder

1 tsp ground turmeric

1 chicken stock cube

800ml coconut water

basil, roughly chopped, to serve

Melt the coconut oil in a large, high-sided frying pan or wok over a medium to high heat, then add the garlic, lemongrass, star anise, chillies, ginger, the finely chopped stalks of the coriander and the spring onions. Stir-fry the ingredients for 2 minutes, then turn up the heat and slide in the chicken.

Continue to stir-fry all the ingredients together for 2 minutes, then add the baby sweetcorn, mange tout and udon noodles. Toss everything together for 1 minute.

Sprinkle in the curry powder and the turmeric and toss to incorporate. Crumble in the stock cube and pour in the coconut water. Bring the whole lot to the boil, then sprinkle over the chopped basil.

Divide the soup between two bowls and serve.

* This recipe requires the stalks from a bunch of coriander. Make sure you save the leaves for another recipe.

Chicken tostadas

* Serves 2

4 medium tortillas (about 15cm)
2 tbsp olive oil
2 x 180g skinless chicken breasts
1 large red onion
juice of 2 fat limes
1 baby gem lettuce, trimmed and shredded
¼ cucumber, de-seeded and cut into 1cm pieces
1 red chilli, de-seeded and finely chopped
400g kidney beans, drained and rinsed
½ bunch of coriander, roughly chopped
salt and black pepper

Preheat the oven to 200°C (fan 180°C/gas mark 6).

Lay your tortillas on two flat baking trays, making sure they don't overlap. If using a brush, then brush over the faintest covering of olive oil on one side.

Slide the trays into your oven and bake for 10 minutes, by which time the tortillas will have browned a little and should be nice and crisp. Remove and leave to cool.

While the tostadas are baking, put each chicken breast between two pieces of cling film, and using a rolling pin, lightly beat until slightly thinned to an even thickness. Brush each side with olive oil and cook on a hot griddle pan for 6–8 minutes on each side, until cooked through. Check by slicing into the chicken to make sure the meat is white all the way through, with no raw pink bits left. Leave to one side to cool, then chop into 1cm strips.

Mix together all of the remaining ingredients with the cooked chicken and season with a little salt and pepper.

Overlap two tostadas on each plate and pile up the topping.

* You could use an oil-spray bottle to give the tortillas the faintest covering of oil before they are baked. Just give each tortilla a couple of pumps on one side.

CHICKEN & MUSHROOM
risotto

* Serves 4
* Make ahead
* Freeze ahead

12g dried porcini mushrooms

2 chicken stock cubes

1 tbsp coconut oil

1 large leek, trimmed, washed and finely chopped

5 sprigs of thyme

400g skinless and boneless chicken thighs, cut into 2cm pieces

300g mushrooms, brushed clean and roughly chopped into 2cm chunks

225g arborio rice

small bunch of parsley, roughly chopped

small bunch of chives, finely chopped

juice of 1 lemon

salt and black pepper

Pour enough boiling water over the dried mushrooms to cover them generously, then leave to soak. Drop the stock cubes into a jug and, using boiling water, make up 750ml of stock.

Melt half of the oil in a large saucepan over a medium to high heat, then slide in the leek and thyme. Stir and cook for 2 minutes, then cover and leave to sweat for 2 minutes.

Take the lid off and crank up the heat to maximum. Add the chicken thigh pieces and a third of the chopped mushrooms. Cook, stirring every now and again, for 2 minutes. Slide in the rice and stir in to combine with the other ingredients.

Drain the sodden mushrooms and leave to one side, measuring out 150ml of the liquid. Pour the liquid into the pan with the sodden mushrooms and allow it to bubble up.

For the next 20 minutes, add a ladleful of the stock at a time to the rice, while constantly stirring. Don't add too much stock to the pan otherwise you will lower the heat, which increases the cooking time. After 20 minutes you should have incorporated all of the stock into the pan, and you should be looking down at a creamy risotto – the rice should be just soft to the bite.

Put a lid on and leave the risotto to sit for a couple of minutes.

Meanwhile, melt the remaining oil in a large frying pan over a high heat, then add the remaining mushrooms. Fry without turning for 1 minute to caramelize.

Add the mushrooms to the risotto along with the chopped parsley, chives and lemon juice. Stir, taste for seasoning then serve.

CHICKEN & SAFFRON

ragu

* Serves 4
* Make ahead
* Freeze ahead

½ tbsp coconut oil

1 large red onion, peeled and diced

3 cloves garlic, finely chopped

5 sprigs of thyme

6 boneless and skinless chicken thighs (600g), each cut into 4 large chunks

300g wholemeal fusilli pasta

8g tomato puree

small pinch of saffron

75ml red wine

250ml passata

large bunch of basil, roughly chopped

50g pitted black olives, roughly chopped

Put a large pan of water on to boil.

Melt the oil in a large, high-sided frying pan over a medium to high heat, and when it is melted and hot, add the red onion, garlic and thyme and fry, stirring regularly for 5 minutes until the onions have softened.

Crank up the heat to maximum and add the chopped chicken thighs to the pan. Without letting the other ingredients burn, try not to stir the meat too much so that it has the chance to brown a little in places. Cook the chicken for about 2 minutes – your aim here is not to cook it through.

This is probably a good time to drop the pasta into the boiling water to cook.

Squeeze in the tomato puree, add the saffron and mix the whole lot together, frying and stirring for about 1 minute.

Pour in the wine and let it bubble, then add the passata and bring it up to a simmer. Cook the ragu like this for about 10 minutes, or until you are happy the chicken is fully cooked through. Check by slicing into the chicken to make sure the meat is white all the way through, with no raw pink bits left.

If you feel the pan is cooking dry, then just scoop out a little of the pasta cooking water and add to the pan.

When the pasta is done and you're happy the chicken is cooked through, drain the pasta then tip it straight into the pan with the sauce.

Add the basil and olives and stir to combine everything.

HARISSA & RED PEPPER
roast chicken

* Serves 4
* Longer recipe
* Make ahead

1 tbsp coconut oil

8 chicken thighs, bone-in and skin-on

1½ tbsp harissa paste

2 fennel bulbs, trimmed and cut into chunky lengths

2 red onions, peeled and cut into wedges

2 red peppers, de-seeded and cut into 3cm chunks

6 tbsp yoghurt

1 tbsp chives, chopped

½ small bunch of parsley, roughly chopped

salt and black pepper

steamed greens, to serve

Preheat the oven to 200°C (fan 180°C/gas mark 6).

Dollop the coconut oil into a heavy-based roasting tray and slide into the oven to melt for 5 minutes.

Tip the chicken thighs into a bowl and spoon over the harissa. Get your hands stuck in and smear the meat all over with the hot paste.

After 5 minutes, slide the tray out and carefully lay the chicken thighs in the hot fat, skin-side down. Tumble all the prepped veg over the top of the chicken, then slide the tray back into the oven. The tray should be crammed with ingredients. Roast for 30 minutes.

After 30 minutes, using a couple of forks or tongs carefully pull the chicken from under the veg and place it on top, skin-side up. Repeat the process with all of the chicken thighs, then slide the tray back into the oven and roast for a further 25 minutes, until you have a tray of lovely caramelized chicken on top of tender vegetables.

Mix together the yoghurt, chives and parsley along with a good pinch of both salt and pepper.

Serve up the chicken and veg with steamed greens and a dollop of the herby yoghurt.

Chicken & miso
NOODLE SOUP

* Serves 2

1 sachet of miso powder
or paste

½ tbsp coconut oil

2 cloves garlic, finely chopped

3cm ginger, peeled and finely
chopped

1 x 300g skinless chicken
breast, cut into 1cm slices

150g oyster mushrooms, large
ones, torn in half

2 pak choy, cut into 4 pieces
lengthways

300g fresh egg noodles

2 small handfuls of bean sprouts

2 spring onions, finely sliced

1½ tbsp light soy sauce

Bring a kettle to the boil and dilute the miso powder or paste with 500ml of boiling water. Leave to one side.

Melt the oil in a large frying pan or wok over a medium to high heat, then add the garlic and ginger and stir-fry for 30 seconds. Add the chicken and continue to stir-fry the ingredients together for 3 minutes. Add the mushrooms and pak choy. Fry all together for 2–3 minutes, or until the chicken and the mushrooms are lightly browned and virtually cooked through.

Drop the noodles in and give them a toss together with all the other cooking ingredients.

Turn down the heat a little and pour in the miso. Slowly bring the liquid up to the boil and simmer for 1 minute.

Serve up the noodles topped with the bean sprouts, spring onions and the soy sauce.

MAKE IT VEG
Replace the chicken with the same quantity of tofu, either silken or firm. Simply chuck it in with the miso and simmer for 5 minutes.

Paprika chicken
WITH APPLE & DILL SLAW

* Serves 4

2 tbsp olive oil

2 tsp sweet smoked paprika

1 tsp onion granules

1 tsp celery salt

12 skinless and boneless chicken thighs

½ small red cabbage (300g), core removed

1 carrot, peeled and cut into matchsticks (100g)

1 apple, peeled and cored and cut into matchsticks (100g)

small bunch of dill, finely chopped

4 spring onions, trimmed and finely chopped

75g mayonnaise

60g pecans, roughly chopped

Preheat the oven to 200°C (fan 180°C/gas mark 6).

Pour the oil into a large sandwich bag and add the paprika, onion granules and celery salt. Mix together, then add the chicken thighs, seal the bag and give the whole lot a good squidge around to ensure the chicken is evenly coated in the spiced oil.

Tip the thighs onto a baking tray and roast in the oven for 25 minutes, or until you are certain the chicken is fully cooked through. You can check by slicing into one of the larger pieces to make sure the meat is white all the way through, with no raw pink bits left.

While the chicken is cooking, mix together all the remaining ingredients to make a tasty coleslaw.

Serve up the chicken on top of a pile of coleslaw.

* You can make the slaw ahead, but squeeze it with a little lemon juice to stop the apple from browning.

CHICKEN & ORZO
rat-a-tat bake

* Serves 4
* Make ahead
* Freeze ahead

1 tbsp coconut oil

1 red onion, peeled and diced

1 courgette, trimmed and diced (250g)

1 aubergine, trimmed and diced (250g)

4 sprigs of fresh oregano

4 sprigs of fresh thyme

3 cloves garlic, finely chopped

1 tbsp tomato puree

250g orzo

1 x 400g tin of chopped tomatoes

250ml chicken stock

2 x 200g chicken breasts, cut into 1cm slices

1 tsp sweet smoked paprika

salt and black pepper

small bunch of parsley, roughly chopped

small bunch of chives, finely chopped

Preheat the oven to 200°C (fan 180°C/gas mark 6).

Melt half of the oil in a heavy-based flameproof casserole dish over a medium to high heat. Add the onion and cook for 1 minute, then throw in the courgette, aubergine, oregano, thyme and 2 chopped garlic cloves. Fry, stirring regularly for 5 minutes, until the vegetables are starting to soften.

Add the tomato puree and orzo and mix to combine. Pour in the chopped tomatoes and chicken stock and bring the mixture quickly to the boil, stirring regularly. Put the lid on and slide the dish into the oven.

Meanwhile, melt the remaining oil in a large frying pan over a high heat. Add the sliced chicken and the remaining chopped garlic clove. Stir-fry the chicken so that it is virtually cooked through – it is more important at this stage to colour the meat than to cook it through.

Sprinkle in the paprika along with a pinch of salt and pepper and toss the whole lot together.

Remove the pasta from the oven and carefully take off the lid, stir in the chicken, slide the lid back on and bake the whole lot together for 10 more minutes.

After 10 minutes, take the dish from the oven and stir through the parsley and chives. Serve straight from the dish to the masses.

WEST COAST QUINOA
chicken bowl

* Serves 2
* Make ahead

1 x 300g skinless chicken breast

2–3 tsp olive oil

250g pre-cooked quinoa – red and white mixed

1 x 400g tin of black beans, drained and rinsed

2 tbsp pomegranate molasses

1½ tbsp white wine vinegar

3 spring onions, trimmed and finely sliced

¼ small red cabbage, shredded

16 cherries, de-stoned and halved

1 carrot, peeled and grated

small bunch of coriander, to serve

Put the chicken breast between two pieces of cling film, and using a rolling pin, lightly beat until slightly thinned to an even thickness. Brush each side with olive oil and cook on a hot griddle pan for 6–8 minutes on each side, until cooked through. Check by slicing into the chicken to make sure the meat is white all the way through, with no raw pink bits left.

Ping the quinoa in the microwave according to the packet instructions, then tip into a bowl and stir through the beans immediately. Leave to sit.

Mix together the pomegranate molasses with the vinegar and keep to one side. Shred the chicken breast.

Stir the sliced spring onions and half of the molasses dressing through the warm quinoa and bean mix, then divide between two bowls. Top the bowls with the cabbage, cherries, carrot and shredded chicken, then drizzle over the remaining dressing.

Finish with a scattering of chopped coriander.

GRIDDLED
Caesar Niçoise

* Serves 2

4 large spring onions, each trimmed and cut into 3 long batons

8 midget trees (tenderstem broccoli), cut in half lengthways

80g green beans, trimmed

20ml olive oil

salt and black pepper

2 x 180–200g chicken breasts

3 sprigs of thyme, leaves only

1 lemon

60g mayonnaise

10g jarred anchovies, drained and roughly chopped

15g parmesan, grated

2 baby gem lettuces, leaves separated

50g pitted black olives (I like the slightly dried Crespo ones for this)

Put a large griddle pan on to heat over a high flame and fling open some windows – this could get a bit smoky.

Put the spring onions, midget trees and green beans into a bowl and pour in half of the olive oil, along with a good pinch of salt and pepper. Toss the ingredients in the oil to season, then when the griddle is hot, carefully lay on the slicked vegetables and cook, turning regularly for 6 minutes, or until just cooked through. Remove and keep to one side.

While the vegetables are cooking, take each chicken breast one at a time and slice into the thick side, cutting almost but not all the way through. Open the breast up like a book and push down on it with the palm of your hand to flatten the meat a little. Place the prepared chicken breast in a bowl and repeat the process with the second breast.

Pour the remaining oil over the chicken breasts and add the thyme leaves, the juice of half of the lemon and a good pinch of salt, then roughly swish the meat around the bowl to coat it with the flavours.

-7

GRIDDLED
Caesar Niçoise

(continued)

When the griddle is clear of the veg, lay the breasts on and griddle for 3–4 minutes on each side, or until you are sure the meat is cooked through. Check by slicing into one of the thicker pieces to make sure the meat is white all the way through, with no raw pink bits left. Remove the chicken to a plate and leave to rest a little.

Blitz the mayonnaise, anchovies, parmesan and the juice of the remaining lemon half until smooth. (Depending on how much juice comes from the lemon, you may or may not need to add a splash of water to the dressing.)

Divide the salad leaves over two plates, then arrange the cooked veg over the top. Slice the chicken into strips and add to the plates. Finish with a few black olives and a good drizzling of the dressing.

You can make all the salad components ahead, then toss them together just before serving.

FENNEL & RADISH
chicken noodles

* Serves 2

½ tbsp coconut oil

1 large fennel bulb, trimmed and finely sliced

8 radishes, trimmed and finely sliced

4 spring onions, trimmed and finely sliced

3 cloves garlic, finely sliced

2 x 180g chicken breasts, cut into 1cm strips

4 baby sweetcorn, cut into thin rounds

300g fresh egg noodles

1½ tbsp light soy sauce

Melt the coconut oil in a large frying pan over a medium to high heat, then chuck in the fennel and radishes and stir-fry for 2 minutes.

Add the spring onions and garlic and continue to stir-fry for a further minute.

Crank up the heat to maximum, then slide in the chicken pieces and stir-fry for about 3 minutes. Check by slicing into one of the pieces to make sure the meat is white all the way through, with no raw pink bits left. If you feel the ingredients are burning before the chicken is cooked, pour in about 2 tablespoons of water and let it steam up.

Add the sweetcorn and noodles and toss to mix all the ingredients together. Add a couple more tablespoons of water to warm the noodles.

Turn the heat off, stir through the soy sauce and serve up.

CHICKEN & SQUID
orzo paella

* Serves 4
* Make ahead
* Freeze ahead

1 chicken stock cube
pinch of saffron
1½ tbsp coconut oil
2 red onions, peeled and diced
1 red pepper, de-seeded and cut into thin slices
3 cloves garlic, chopped
5 medium tomatoes (320g), roughly chopped
10g tomato puree
300g orzo
¼ tsp smoked paprika
125g frozen peas
300g baby squid, cleaned and prepped
2 x 200g chicken breasts, cut into 1cm-thick slices
large bunch of parsley, roughly chopped
2 lemons, cut into quarters, to serve

Put a kettle on to boil and preheat the oven to 200°C (fan 180°C/gas mark 6).

Pour 500ml boiling water over the chicken stock cube and add the saffron. Leave to steep.

Melt 1 tablespoon of the coconut oil over a high heat in a large ovenproof pan or flameproof casserole dish, then add the chopped onions, red pepper and garlic and stir-fry for 5 minutes.

Stir in the fresh tomatoes and the tomato puree and continue to stir-fry for a further 5 minutes, until the tomatoes begin to break down. Stir in the orzo, paprika and frozen peas, and finally pour in the infused chicken stock along with the bits of saffron. Bring the liquid to the boil, clamp on a lid and slide the pan or dish into the oven. Bake for 15 minutes.

While the orzo is cooking, take the baby squid tubes and cut them in half lengthways. Score the inside of the flesh at 5mm intervals in one direction, then turn 45 degrees and score again to create a diamond pattern. Repeat the scoring with the remaining squid.

→

* It's not totally necessary to score the squid, but it looks good and helps to keep it tender.

CHICKEN & SQUID

orzo paella

(continued)

Melt half of the remaining coconut oil in a large frying pan over a high heat, then fry the chicken for about 4 minutes or until you are happy it's totally cooked through. Try not to stir the meat too much to allow it to brown.

Scrape the chicken out of the pan into a waiting bowl, wipe the frying pan with a piece of kitchen roll and place straight back onto the heat with the remaining coconut oil. Melt the oil until it is blisteringly hot, then carefully add the squid and stir-fry for about 2 minutes, or until just cooked through.

Remove the paella from the oven, carefully take off the lid then top with the fried chicken and squid. Finish with a generous scattering of chopped parsley and lemon wedges.

Chicken & brussels

WITH PASTA SHELLS

* Serves 2

200g pasta shells
½ tbsp coconut oil
pinch of dried chilli flakes
zest and juice of 1 lemon
4 cloves garlic, finely chopped
1 fresh red chilli, finely sliced –
remove the seeds if you don't
like it hot
1 x 300g chicken breast, cut into
1cm slices
250g brussels sprouts, trimmed
and shredded
salt and black pepper
bunch of parsley, roughly
chopped

Put a large pot of water on to boil, and when boiling, cook your pasta according to packet instructions. Just before draining the pasta, scoop out half a mugful of the starchy cooking liquid and keep to one side.

While the pasta is cooking, melt the coconut oil in a large frying pan over a medium to high heat. When the oil is melted and hot, add the chilli flakes, zest of lemon, garlic and fresh chilli. Fry, stirring regularly for 2 minutes, then add the chicken pieces and the brussels sprouts and crank up the heat to maximum. Stir-fry the ingredients all together for about 6 minutes, by which time the brussels should be lightly browned and the chicken pretty much cooked through. Reduce the heat to very low.

Having scooped out some of the water, drain the pasta through a colander then tip into the pan with the chicken. Splash in some of the cooking liquid then add the lemon juice, a good pinch of salt and pepper and the parsley. Toss the whole lot together and enjoy.

BANG BANG
chicken stir-fry

* Serves 4

1 tbsp coconut oil

2 star anise

3 cloves garlic, finely chopped

6 spring onions, trimmed and finely sliced

1 tsp Sichuan peppercorns

3 x 200g chicken breasts, cut into 1cm slices

4 pak choy, cut into quarters lengthways

200g midget trees (tenderstem broccoli), cut in half lengthways

120g baby sweetcorn, cut in half lengthways

500g fresh egg noodles

½ tsp hot smoked paprika

½ tbsp light soy sauce

Melt the oil in a large frying pan or wok over a high heat. Add the star anise and fry for a few seconds, then quickly follow with the garlic, spring onions and Sichuan peppercorns. Stir-fry for 30 seconds.

Tip in the chicken, stirring every now and again so that the meat browns a little, about 2 minutes. Add the pak choy and midget trees and stir-fry for about 3 minutes. Add 2 tablespoons of water to the pan to steam up and cook everything through.

Add the sweetcorn and egg noodles and continue to stir-fry for a couple more minutes until everything is steaming hot.

Take the pan off the heat and add the paprika and soy sauce, tossing the whole lot together to ensure even coverage.

Divide between four plates and enjoy.

Watermelon & chicken

WITH GLASS NOODLES

* Serves 4
* Make ahead

4 x 180–200g skinless
chicken breasts

½ tbsp coconut oil

3 cloves garlic, roughly chopped

2 lemongrass stalks, tender
white part only, finely chopped

2 red chillies, de-seeded and
finely chopped

2 kaffir lime leaves

2 large, very ripe tomatoes,
chopped into 2cm chunks

600g fresh glass noodles
(sometimes called vermicelli)

¼ cucumber, de-seeded and cut
into half-moons

4 spring onions, trimmed and
finely sliced

2 tbsp fish sauce

juice of 3 limes

½ small watermelon, flesh
only, cut into large chunks
(roughly 500g)

bunch of coriander, roughly
chopped

Bring a large pan of water to the boil. When the water is bubbling, gently lay the chicken breasts in the pan and turn the heat down to its lowest setting. Cook the chicken very gently for 12 minutes, then turn the heat off and leave the breasts to sit in the water to keep warm until you're ready to eat.

Melt the coconut oil in a saucepan over a medium to low heat, then add the garlic, lemongrass, chillies, lime leaves and tomatoes. Cook the ingredients slowly for 10 minutes until the tomatoes start to break down a little.

While the chicken and sauce are cooking, bring a kettle to the boil, drop the noodles into a sieve and pour the hot water over the noodles. Follow the hot water with cold water to cool the noodles back down again. Tip the noodles into a large bowl.

Turn the heat off under the tomato pan, then add the cucumber, spring onions, fish sauce and lime juice. Stir to combine everything.

Chuck the tomato dressing into the noodles along with the watermelon pieces. Carefully remove the chicken from the hot water, and using a combination of two forks, shred the meat into small pieces and add these to the large bowl, too.

Add half of the chopped coriander and toss everything gently together.

Serve up the salad sprinkled with the remaining coriander.

Chicken, kale & brussels

* Serves 4

½ tbsp coconut oil

1 onion, peeled and diced

75g smoked streaky bacon, cut into 1cm strips

1 x 300g skinless chicken breast, cut into 1cm strips

190g brussels sprouts, trimmed and shredded

50g kale, thick stalks removed

100g pre-cooked chestnuts, crumbled

80g taleggio or mozzarella

2 red chillies, de-seeded and finely sliced

Melt the coconut oil in a large frying pan over a medium to high heat, then add the onion and chopped bacon. Fry for 2–3 minutes until the bacon is browned and crisp. Slide in the chicken breast and cook for about 4 minutes until it is just cooked through.

Add the brussels and the kale and crank up the heat to maximum. Stir-fry the whole lot together for 2 minutes, then add a splash of water, which will steam up and help to cook the chicken and greens.

Turn on your grill to maximum.

Take the mix off the heat and scatter with the chestnut pieces. Cut the taleggio into rough slices and dot all over. Slide under the hot grill and cook for 2 minutes until the taleggio is just melted.

Finish with a sprinkling of red chilli and serve up.

LIME & CHORIZO
chicken legs

* Serves 4
* Make ahead
* Freeze ahead

12 chicken drumsticks
drizzle of olive oil
salt and black pepper
30g honey
3 limes
20ml soy sauce
8 small cooking chorizo
4 baby gem lettuces, cut in quarters lengthways
8 radishes, thinly sliced
50g toasted cashews, roughly chopped

Preheat the oven to 200°C (fan 180°C/gas mark 6).

Tumble the chicken legs into a roasting tray, drizzle over a little oil and sprinkle with salt and pepper. Slide straight into the hot oven and cook for 15 minutes.

Meanwhile, mix together the honey, juice of three limes and the zest of one and the soy sauce in a bowl.

After 15 minutes take the roasting tray out of the oven and add the chorizo. Pour over the lime dressing and toss the whole lot together. Put the tray back into the oven and cook for a further 15 minutes.

After 15 minutes, everything should be nicely cooked through. You can check the chicken by slicing into one of the drumsticks to make sure the meat is white all the way through, with no raw pink bits left.

Serve up the baby gem lettuce, top with the chicken and chorizo and spoon over some of the cooking juices.

Finish with the sliced radish and cashews.

Photo overleaf

Dukkah-spiced chicken
WITH GIANT COUSCOUS & POMEGRANATE DRESSING

* Serves 4
* Make ahead

250g giant couscous
4 x 180–200g skinless
chicken breasts
100g dukkah mix
1 tbsp coconut oil
5 radishes, roughly chopped
½ cucumber, de-seeded and cut
into half-moons
1 jarred red pepper, drained
and cut into 2cm strips
½ red onion, peeled and
finely diced
bunch of parsley, roughly
chopped
2½ tbsp pomegranate molasses
1½ tbsp white wine vinegar
pomegranate seeds,
to serve – optional

Bring a large pot of water to the boil and cook the couscous according to packet instructions. Drain through a sieve and cool down with cold running water. Give it a shake to drain well and tip it into a large bowl.

While the couscous is cooking, take each chicken breast one at a time and slice into the thick side, cutting almost but not all the way through. Open the breast up like a book and push down on it with the palm of your hand to flatten the meat a little. Place the prepared chicken breast in a bowl and repeat the process with the remaining breasts.

Scatter the dukkah onto a plate and then, taking one breast at a time, push it into the mix, sticking as much of the mix to the flesh as you can. Repeat the process with the remaining breasts.

It is likely you will have to cook the breasts two at a time, so melt half of the coconut oil in a large non-stick frying pan over a medium to high heat. Gently lay the two breasts into the hot fat and fry for 3–4 minutes on each side until the chicken is just cooked through. Check by slicing into one of the thicker pieces to make sure the meat is white all the way through, with no raw pink bits left.

Take the chicken from the pan and lightly rub it with kitchen roll, then wipe the pan out and repeat the process with the remaining oil and chicken breasts.

Add the radishes, cucumber, red pepper, red onion and parsley to the couscous. Mix the pomegranate molasses together with the vinegar, then toss the dressing through the couscous salad.

Serve up the couscous with the spiced chicken and a scattering of pomegranate seeds (if using).

BACON-WRAPPED, CHEESE-STUFFED
chicken breasts

* Serves 4

4 × 200g chicken breasts

170g garlic and herb cheese
(I use Le Roule)

12 rashers of smoked streaky
bacon

½ tbsp coconut oil

3 baby gem lettuces, quartered
lengthways

2 avocados, de-stoned and
cut into wedges

16 cherry tomatoes, sliced
in half

salt and black pepper

1 tbsp balsamic vinegar

1 tbsp olive oil

Preheat the oven to 200°C (fan 180°C/gas mark 6).

Take each breast in turn and cut down the entire length of the breast, ensuring you don't cut all the way through. Using a short scoring motion, open up the sides a little to create a pocket shape. Repeat the process with the other chicken breasts.

Spread a quarter of the cheese into the pocket you've created in each of the chicken breasts, trying to keep it as even as possible. Gently squeeze the flesh together, then wrap each of the breasts in three rashers of bacon, keeping the rashers tight without overlapping them.

Melt the coconut oil in a large ovenproof frying pan over a medium to high heat, then gently place the breasts in, join-side down. Fry the breasts for about 3 minutes on each side or until the bacon has turned a nice brown colour. Slide the pan into your oven and cook for 15 minutes or until you are happy the chicken is cooked all the way through – you can check this by cutting into the thickest part of the breast and ensuring the meat has turned white, with no raw pink bits left.

While the chicken is cooking, toss together the baby gem wedges, sliced avocados and cherry tomatoes. Season with a little salt and pepper, then add the balsamic vinegar and olive oil and toss gently again.

Divide the salad between four plates and top with the cooked chicken breasts.

Chipotle chicken
ORANGE & WATERCRESS SALAD

* Serves 2

1½ tbsp coconut oil
6 chicken thighs, bone-in and skin-on
2½ tbsp chipotle paste
salt
1 large red onion, peeled and cut into 12 wedges
1 orange
2 large handfuls of watercress
a couple of drizzles of olive oil
40g walnuts, roughly chopped

Preheat the oven to 220°C (fan 200°C/gas mark 7). Dollop the coconut oil onto a roasting tray and slide into the oven to melt and heat up for 5 minutes.

Place the chicken thighs in a bowl and spoon on the chipotle paste. Give the meat a good swoosh around to evenly coat the thighs. Season generously with salt.

Remove the tray from the oven and quickly but carefully lay the thighs in the hot fat, skin-side down. Tumble the red onion wedges around the chicken and roast the whole lot together for 15 minutes.

Remove the tray and flip the thighs up the other way round and roast for a final 10 minutes.

While the thighs are roasting, peel the orange and cut into slices across its diameter, each slice just thicker than a pound coin.

Serve up the watercress, nestling in the orange slices, and drizzle with a little olive oil. Pile up the chicken thighs, then scatter with the chopped walnuts.

* You can make all the components ahead, then assemble them just before serving.

Roast chicken
WITH BUTTERNUT, FIGS & GOAT'S CHEESE

* Serves 4

1 tbsp coconut oil

1 medium butternut squash, peeled, de-seeded and cut into 2cm cubes (425g)

4 sprigs of thyme, leaves only

4 x 180g chicken breasts, skin-on

6 figs, quartered lengthways

75g soft goat's cheese

40g walnuts, roughly chopped

drizzle of balsamic vinegar

4 handfuls of rocket

Preheat the oven to 210°C (fan 190°C/gas mark 6–7).

Dollop half of the coconut oil onto a baking tray. Drop the chopped butternut squash onto the tray, toss through the thyme leaves then slide the tray into the oven to roast for 20 minutes.

In the meantime, melt the remaining oil in a frying pan over a medium heat, then lay the chicken breasts in the pan, skin-side down. Fry the chicken breasts for about 7 minutes only on the skin side, by which time they should be dark brown. Flip over and cook for a couple of minutes on the other side.

Take your roasting squash from the oven and give it a toss. Lay the chicken on top of the butternut cubes, skin-side up. Dot around the fig quarters and then slide the tray back into your hot oven for a final 10-minute blast.

The chicken should be perfectly cooked through. Check by slicing into one of the thicker pieces of breast to make sure the meat is white all the way through, with no raw pink bits left.

Plate up the chicken, butternut and figs, dot with goat's cheese, then sprinkle over the chopped walnuts and a drizzle of balsamic. Serve with rocket.

You can make all the components ahead, then assemble them just before serving.

Fish
& Seafood

EDAMAME, PINK GINGER &
smoked salmon salad

* Serves 2

150g podded edamame beans
(400g un-podded)

1 courgette, trimmed and
washed

6 radishes, finely sliced

20g pickled pink ginger, drained
and roughly chopped

2 tsp sesame oil

4 tsp rice wine vinegar

2 tsp light soy sauce

225g smoked salmon

black sesame seeds, to serve

Tip the edamame beans into a bowl. Take your courgette and, using a peeler, create long thin ribbons along the entire length of the courgette. When you get close to the core, rotate the courgette and continue on the other side. You won't be able to make ribbons with the whole courgette, so just keep what's left of the core for another recipe, such as a stir-fry.

Add the courgette strips to the edamame along with the sliced radishes.

Mix together the pickled ginger, sesame oil, vinegar and soy sauce in a bowl and pour it over the vegetables. Give the whole lot a toss together, then stack up over two plates. Top with the smoked salmon and sprinkle with black sesame seeds.

Tuna & egg bruschetta

* Serves 2

180g green beans, trimmed
4 slices of thick crusty bread
drizzle of olive oil
1 fat clove garlic
1 large, very ripe tomato, cut in half
2 tsp coconut oil
2 × 140g tuna steaks
salt and black pepper
9 pitted black olives, cut in half
5 sundried tomatoes, drained and patted dry
2 hard-boiled eggs

Bring a pot of water to the boil and when simmering, cook the beans for 3 minutes, or until just cooked through. Drain and leave to one side.

Drizzle the bread with a little olive oil on both sides. Heat a grill over a high heat, and when smoking hot, lay the bread down carefully and cook for 2 minutes on each side until crisp and dark golden.

Remove the bread and immediately rub with the garlic. The bread's rough surface acts as a grater, which wears the garlic down into the bread. Do the same with the tomato, pushing and smudging it into the bread. Leave the bread to one side.

Melt the oil in a frying pan over a high heat. Season the tuna steaks with salt and pepper and carefully lay them in the hot oil. Fry for about 90 seconds on each side, then remove to a plate.

Mix the beans with the olives, sundried tomatoes and a splash of olive oil. Toss together, seasoning as you go.

Slice the tuna into strips. Pile the beans on top of the bread, slice up the eggs and arrange them on top of the beans, then finish with the tuna strips.

* This is a classic breakfast in Spain.
  The key is to use good bread and slightly overripe tomatoes.

Shallot & fennel

WITH GRILLED SEA BASS

* Serves 2

50ml olive oil
1 tsp fennel seeds
3 banana shallots, peeled and
sliced finely lengthways (150g)
2 fennel bulbs, trimmed and
finely sliced
75ml white wine
4 x 100g sea bass fillets
1 lemon
pea shoots, to serve

You'll need a medium saucepan with a tight-fitting lid for this. Heat the oil in the medium saucepan over a medium to high heat. When the oil is hot, add the fennel seeds and fry for about 30 seconds, then add the shallots and fennel. Crank up the heat to maximum and fry the vegetables for 3 minutes, stirring frequently.

Pour in the wine, allowing it to steam up, then turn down the heat to medium and clamp on a lid. Cook the fennel and shallots, stirring intermittently for 20 minutes, by which time they will be lightly browned but also meltingly tender.

While the veg is stewing, heat the grill to its highest setting. Using a sharp knife, make about four cuts in the skin of the sea bass then sprinkle liberally with salt. Lay the fillets, skin-side up, on a flat tray and cook on the skin side only for 6 minutes, by which time the fish will be cooked through and the skin crisp and slightly blistered in places. Turn off the heat and shut the grill door.

Just before serving, squeeze half a lemon's worth of juice into the fennel and shallots and stir through. Serve up mounds of the fennel and shallots, topped with the fish fillets, a handful of pea shoots and a wedge of lemon.

Sambal sea bass

WITH BAKED COCONUT RICE

* Serves 4

½ tbsp coconut oil

5 large shallots, peeled and diced

7 cloves garlic, roughly chopped

4 cardamom pods, bruised with the side of a knife

275g basmati or jasmine rice

1 chicken stock cube

500ml coconut water

7cm ginger, peeled and roughly chopped

2 lemongrass stalks, tender white part only, finely sliced

1 tbsp fish sauce

5 red chillies, roughly chopped – remove the seeds if you don't like it hot

juice of 1 lime

8 x 100g skinless sea bass fillets

coriander, to serve

Preheat the oven to 190°C (fan 170°C/gas mark 5).

Melt the coconut oil in a large flameproof casserole dish over a medium to high heat, then add 2 diced shallots, 1 clove of chopped garlic and the cardamom pods and fry for 2 minutes.

Tip in the rice and stir to mix with the other ingredients, then crumble in the stock cube. Pour in the coconut water and bring to a boil. Put a lid on the pan and slide it into your hot oven. Bake for 15 minutes.

While the rice is cooking, blitz together the remaining shallots, garlic, ginger, lemongrass, fish sauce, chillies and lime juice. You might have to add a little water to get them started. Smother the sea bass with all but about 3 tablespoons of the sauce. You aren't looking to totally cover the fish, just roughly coat it.

Lay the fish carefully on a baking tray lined with baking parchment, then cook under a hot grill for 5 minutes without turning. The marinade and fish may darken in places, but don't worry.

As soon as the rice and fish are cooked, serve them with a dollop of the reserved sambal sauce and sprigs of coriander.

Tandoori cod burgers
WITH SWEET POTATO FRIES

* Serves 2

2 large sweet potatoes (600g),
scrubbed clean

2 tsp olive oil

salt and black pepper

40ml rice vinegar

2g caster sugar

1 red chilli, de-seeded and
finely sliced

¼ red onion, finely sliced

¼ cucumber (80g), de-seeded
and cut into thin half-moons

2 x 200g skinless and boneless
cod fillets

30g tikka masala curry paste

2 burger buns

To serve

1 tbsp fat-free Greek yoghurt

1 tomato, thinly sliced

1 tbsp coriander, chopped

Preheat the oven to 200°C (fan 180°C/gas mark 6).

Cut each sweet potato in half lengthways, then cut into eight long, thin wedges and scatter over one layer on a baking tray. Drizzle over the olive oil along with a good pinch of salt, toss to mix then roast in the oven for 25 minutes.

Mix together the rice vinegar, sugar, red chilli, onion and cucumber in a small bowl and leave to steep, giving it a mix every now and then.

Coat the cod fillets in the curry paste then place onto a baking tray lined with parchment and roast in the oven for 15 minutes, by which time they should be just cooked through. When the fish has only 5 minutes to go, cut the buns in half and place in the oven to toast.

To build the burger, spread a little yoghurt onto two bun halves, load up with sliced tomato, lay the fish on top then scatter the cucumber mix over (drain off the excess vinegar). Finish with the coriander and squash the remaining bun halves on top. Serve with the sweet potato fries.

* Feel free to use any type of white fish or even chicken breast instead of the cod fillets.

Prawn & chorizo skewers

WITH MELON & BASIL

* Serves 4
* Barbecue

4 raw chorizo sausages (225g)

20 large raw prawns, peeled and cleaned

1 sweet charentais melon, peeled and cut into 3cm chunks (900g)

2 avocados, de-stoned and cut into wedges

small bunch of basil, roughly chopped

dash of red wine vinegar

dash of olive oil

salt and black pepper

50g pumpkin seeds

Fire up the barbecue, if using.

Take four large bamboo skewers and leave them to soak in water for 5 minutes.

Cut the chorizo sausages into slices about the thickness of two one-pound coins – you need to end up with 20 slices of chorizo.

To make the skewers, pierce the sharp end through the very tip of a prawn tail, then follow with a slice of chorizo. Curl the prawn around the chorizo and fix firmly by piercing through the top of the prawn. Gently slide the prawn-wrapped chorizo to the base of the skewer and repeat the process four more times, so you end up with five prawns and five thick slices of chorizo on a skewer. Repeat the process with the remaining prawns, chorizo and skewers.

To cook the skewers, lay them on the barbecue or on a large pre-heated griddle pan. Cook for about 4 minutes each side, giving them a press with the back of a spatula as they griddle to ensure even cooking.

While the skewers are cooking, gently mix together all of the remaining ingredients apart from the pumpkin seeds. Season with a tiny pinch of salt and pepper, then divide over four plates. Top each pile of melon salad with a skewer and the pumpkin seeds.

If you're cooking on the griddle you may not have a pan large enough to fit the skewers in, but you could cook in batches or grill the skewers for 4 minutes on each side.

Crab-o-cado Caprese

* Serves 4

2 ripe avocados, de-stoned
juice of 2–3 limes
1½ tbsp olive oil
salt
300g cooked white crabmeat
or prawns
2 red chillies, de-seeded and
finely chopped
bunch of chives, finely chopped
2 large tomatoes (like beef)
2 balls of mozzarella, drained
small bunch of basil, leaves only
30g toasted pine nuts

Scoop the avocado flesh into a bowl and add the lime juice and olive oil along with a good pinch of salt. Using the back of a fork, crush the avocado together with the juice and oil until you have a coarse mix.

Add the crabmeat, chillies and chives and fold them into the crushed avocado.

Slice the tomatoes thinly and divide over four plates. Sprinkle a little salt over the tomato slices. Divide the crab-o-cado over the four plates, then rip up the mozzarella and add that to the plates, too.

Finish with a scattering of basil leaves and pine nuts.

Aubergine korma
WITH SPICED MONKFISH

* Serves 2
* Make ahead
* Freeze ahead

2 tbsp coconut oil

2 onions, peeled and roughly chopped

5 cardamom pods, lightly crushed

1 tsp ground turmeric

1 tsp ground cumin

salt

1 tbsp olive oil

4 × 200g monkfish, cod or pollock fillets

4 cloves garlic, finely chopped

1 green chilli, split lengthways

1 aubergine, trimmed and cut into 2cm cubes

½ tsp ground cinnamon

400ml coconut milk

200ml chicken or veg stock (add 100ml to 'make it veg', see box)

20g ground almonds

To serve
a dollop of yoghurt
1 chilli, de-seeded and sliced
1 tbsp coriander, chopped

Preheat the oven to 210°C (fan 190°C/gas mark 6–7). Line a baking tray with baking parchment.

Melt the coconut oil in a large frying pan over a medium to high heat. Blitz the onions to a smooth puree and then tip into the hot coconut oil along with the cardamom pods. Fry, stirring regularly for 10 minutes, by which time the onions will be meltingly soft and lightly coloured.

While the onions are cooking, sprinkle half of the turmeric and cumin into a large dish along with half a teaspoon of salt and the olive oil. Give the ingredients a good mix to combine, then swish the fish in the mixture until well coated and roast in the oven for 15 minutes.

Add the garlic, green chilli and aubergine to the pan with the onions and stir-fry for 1 minute. Sprinkle in the remaining turmeric and cumin with all the cinnamon and continue to stir-fry for 30 seconds before adding the coconut milk and stock. Bring the whole lot to a simmer and cook for 10–12 minutes, or until the aubergine is just tender.

When the aubergine is tender, stir in the ground almonds.

Serve the aubergine korma topped with the monkfish, a dollop of yoghurt, sliced chilli and a generous sprinkling of chopped coriander.

> **MAKE IT VEG**
> Add a handful of cauliflower florets, trimmed green beans and 2 chopped tomatoes in with the aubergine. Top with toasted pumpkin seeds.

Roast salmon
WITH CHORIZO & ALMONDS

* Serves 4

1 tbsp coconut oil

225g raw chorizo, cut into
3cm pieces

2 red onions, peeled and cut into
thin wedges

2 red peppers, de-seeded and
cut into strips

1 courgette, trimmed and cut
into half-moons

4 × 175g salmon fillets, skin on

50g kale, thick stalks removed

80g blanched almonds

1 lemon, cut into wedges,
to serve

Preheat the oven to 200°C (fan 180°C/gas mark 6). Dollop the coconut oil onto a large roasting tray and slide the tray into the oven to warm up for 5 minutes.

Remove the tray from the oven and carefully lay on it the chorizo, red onions, peppers and courgette, then roast all together in the oven for 15 minutes.

Remove the tray from the oven, give all the ingredients a bit of a turn and lay the salmon on top, skin-side up. Scatter on the kale and then finally the blanched almonds, and bake in the oven for a final 10 minutes.

Serve up over four plates along with a good wedge of lemon.

Smoked haddock

BAKED ORZO

* Serves 4

1 tbsp coconut oil
2 cloves garlic, finely chopped
2cm ginger, peeled and finely chopped
1 leek, trimmed, washed and finely sliced
1 onion, peeled and diced
200g smoked haddock, skinned and cut into 2cm chunks
250g orzo
1½ tsp curry powder
300ml skimmed milk
200ml fish stock
90g frozen peas
6 eggs
small bunch of chives, to serve

Preheat the oven to 190°C (fan 170°C/gas mark 5).

Melt the coconut oil in a large flameproof casserole dish over a medium to high heat, then add the garlic, ginger, leek and onion and cook, stirring regularly, for 6–7 minutes to soften all the vegetables.

Add the smoked haddock, orzo and curry powder and stir to combine with all the other ingredients.

Pour in the milk, fish stock and peas. Bring up to a simmer, clamp on a lid and slide the dish into the oven. Bake for 10 minutes, then carefully remove it and take off the lid. Use a spoon to make a small hole in the cooking pasta and then crack an egg in. Repeat the process a further five times, then quickly replace the lid and bake for 5 minutes.

Serve up the orzo topped with chopped chives.

Thai cod
IN A BAG

* Serves 4

300ml coconut water

1 fish stock cube

2 lemongrass stalks, bruised with the side of a knife

4 cloves garlic, bashed with your palm

2 bird's eye chillies, split open lengthways

2 kaffir lime leaves

5 spring onions, trimmed and finely sliced

2 tbsp fish sauce

800g skinless cod loin

125g baby sweetcorn, cut in half lengthways

150g midget trees (tenderstem broccoli), thick stalks cut in half lengthways

To serve
small bunch of coriander
small bunch of basil
500g pre-cooked rice

Preheat the oven to 200°C (fan 180°C/gas mark 6).

Heat the coconut water in a saucepan over a low heat. When warm, dissolve the fish stock cube in the coconut water, then add the lemongrass, garlic, chillies, lime leaves and three of the sliced spring onions. Let the ingredients simmer for 3 minutes, then turn off the heat and add the fish sauce.

Roll out a piece of kitchen foil, big enough to cover a large, flat baking tray. Cut off a slightly smaller piece of baking parchment and place in the middle of the foil. Lay the fish in the middle of the paper, then scatter with the sweetcorn and midget trees.

Draw the sides of the foil up a bit around the cod, then carefully pour over the perfumed fish stock, making sure not to lose any over the sides. Finally draw up the foil over the fish to create a large 'tent-like' structure over the ingredients.

Bake the fish in the oven for 15 minutes, then remove and leave to sit for 5 minutes before carefully cutting open (beware the sudden escape of steam when you first cut into the foil).

Sprinkle with the chopped coriander and basil and serve up the fish and sauce on top of steaming rice.

I like using pre-cooked rice, but if you prefer you could cook 170g rice according to packet instructions.

Salmon ceviche

* Serves 2

250g fresh best-quality sushi-
grade skinless salmon

2 tbsp white wine vinegar

1 tsp dijon mustard

25ml olive oil

2 eggs

1 avocado, de-stoned and cut
into thin wedges

6 cherry tomatoes, cut in half

2 small handfuls of watercress

Carefully slice the salmon into eight roughly equal slices, cutting along the length of the flesh. The slices should be about 5mm thick.

Put a pan of water on to boil.

Lay the slices in the centre of two clean plates, then spoon over 1½ tablespoons of the white wine vinegar. Leave the salmon to sit in the vinegar for 15 minutes.

Whisk together the remaining vinegar with the dijon mustard and olive oil, and leave to one side.

Gently lower your eggs into the boiling water and cook for 8 minutes, then immediately drain the hot water and pour over cold water straight from the tap. This not only helps stop the eggs from overcooking, but also makes them easier to peel. Peel the eggs and slice.

When your salmon has had its time in the vinegar, start building your salad by layering up the avocado, cherry tomatoes, egg and avocado slices, then finally a pile of watercress and a drizzle of the dressing.

Grilled mackerel
WITH BEETROOT & POMEGRANATE SLAW

* Serves 2
* Barbecue

2 large mackerel fillets
salt
¼ red cabbage, cored and finely shredded (140g)
2 small cooked beetroot, drained and diced (150g)
30g pomegranate seeds
2 spring onions, sliced
40g mayonnaise
½ small bunch of dill, chopped
40g walnuts, roughly chopped

Fire up the barbecue or preheat your grill to high.

To barbecue the fish without it flaking off, drizzle a little oil on an old, flat baking tray, salt the skin-side of the mackerel then lay on the tray, skin-side up. Put the tray straight onto the hot barbecue then close the lid and cook for anywhere between 5 and 10 minutes, depending on the heat of your barbecue. Don't turn the fish.

If you're grilling in the oven, lay the mackerel fillets on the grill tray skin-side up and sprinkle generously with salt. Slide the fillets under the grill and cook without turning for 6–7 minutes – the skin should blister and darken in places, but also crisp up. The flesh will be perfectly cooked through. Shut the grill door and turn the heat off.

Mix together all of the remaining ingredients, apart from the walnut pieces, to create a dark purple coleslaw. Serve up, topped with the mackerel fillets and a scattering of walnut pieces.

You can make the slaw ahead – it may bleed a little, but it will still taste great.

Soba noodles
WITH TUNA & CUCUMBER

* Serves 2

200g soba noodles
2 pak choy, cut into quarters
lengthways
6cm ginger, peeled
1½ tbsp light soy sauce
1½ tbsp rice wine vinegar
2 tsp sesame oil
¼ cucumber, de-seeded and
cut into half-moons
½ tbsp coconut oil
2 × 175g tuna steaks
2 spring onions, finely sliced

Bring a large pan of water to the boil and add the soba noodles. Cook the noodles according to the packet instructions, but when you have 2 minutes left, add the pak choy.

Drain the noodles and pak choy, then run them under cold water to cool them completely.

Grate the ginger over a clean cloth or fresh piece of kitchen roll. When all the ginger has been grated, gather up the sides of the cloth or paper and gently squeeze the flesh to extract just the juice. You are looking to extract 1½ tablespoons of juice from the flesh. Discard the wrung-out ginger when you have collected the juice.

Add the soy sauce, rice wine vinegar and sesame oil to the ginger juice and stir to mix well. Pour the dressing over the cooled noodles and add the sliced cucumber. Leave the mix to sit while you cook the tuna.

Melt the coconut oil over a high heat in a large non-stick frying pan, then gently lay the tuna steaks in the pan and fry for about 1 minute on each side. Remove the steaks to a plate.

Serve up the soba noodles topped with the tuna and a sprinkling of sliced spring onions.

Photo overleaf

* You can buy soba noodles at the supermarket, but if you can get them from your local Asian store, do so – they will be better quality.

TUNA & AVO
poke bowl

* Serves 2

2 avocados, de-stoned, flesh cut
into rough 1.5cm cubes

325g fresh good-quality sushi-
grade tuna, cut into 2cm chunks

4cm ginger, peeled and
finely chopped

juice of 2 limes

4 spring onions, trimmed and
finely sliced

2½ tsp light soy sauce

1½ tsp sesame oil

1 large baby gem lettuce,
trimmed and shredded

10 cherry tomatoes,
sliced in half

salt

black sesame seeds, to serve

Simply toss all the ingredients – apart from the sesame seeds –
together until well combined. Check for seasoning, adding a little
salt if you think it needs it.

Divide over two plates, then sprinkle with sesame seeds.

Crunchy polenta cod
WITH WHITE BEAN STEW

* Serves 4

1½ tbsp coconut oil

1 red onion, peeled and diced

100g smoked back bacon, all fat trimmed, cut into 1cm strips

1 large carrot, peeled and diced

2 sticks of celery, trimmed and diced

1 tsp fennel seeds

280g cherry tomatoes, sliced in half

400g tin of cannellini beans, drained and rinsed

½ tbsp tomato puree

200ml chicken stock

90g quick-cook polenta

8 × 80g skinless pieces of cod loin

2 big fistfuls of baby spinach leaves

Heat half of the coconut oil in a large high-sided frying pan, and then add the red onion, smoked bacon, carrot, celery and fennel seeds and fry, stirring regularly for 6–7 minutes or until the vegetables are just starting to soften.

Drop in the cherry tomatoes and fry for 2 minutes, or until they just start to lose their shape. Add the beans and the puree and stir to combine everything.

Pour in the stock and bring to the boil. Reduce to a simmer and leave to bubble away for 10 minutes, keeping half an eye on it just in case it runs a bit dry.

While the beans are simmering, tip the polenta onto a plate. Taking each piece of cod one by one, press it into the polenta, ensuring you coat both sides. Lay the crusted piece of fish on a plate and repeat the process with the rest of the fish and the polenta.

When all your pieces of fish are coated, heat up half of the remaining oil in a large non-stick frying pan over a medium to high heat, then gently lay four of the cod pieces in the pan. Fry for about 2 minutes on each side, so that the polenta turns a dark golden yellow and the fish is perfectly steamed through. Remove the cod to a plate, wipe out the frying pan and repeat the process with the remaining oil and coated fish pieces.

Just before serving, stir the spinach leaves through the bean stew, cooking it through until it wilts.

Serve up the stew topped with the crunchy pieces of fish.

Risotto verde

WITH TUNA STEAK

* Serves 2

1 chicken stock cube
1 fish stock cube
1 tbsp coconut oil
1 leek, trimmed and shredded
½ courgette (130g), cut into
1cm dice
225g arborio rice
70g frozen peas
ice cubes
2 × 200g tuna steaks
salt and black pepper
100g watercress
sliced zest of 1 lemon, to serve

Drop the stock cubes into a jug and, using boiling water, make up 900ml of stock.

Melt half of the coconut oil in a large saucepan over a medium to high heat, then add the shredded leek and soften for 3–4 minutes. Add the courgette and rice together and continue to fry for a further 2 minutes.

For the next 20 minutes, add a ladleful of the stock at a time to the rice, while constantly stirring. Don't add too much stock to the pan otherwise you will lower the heat, which increases the cooking time. After 20 minutes you should have incorporated most of the stock into the pan, the rice should be just about cooked and your forearm should be nice and tired. Stir through the frozen peas and turn off the heat.

You're almost there.

Melt the remaining oil in a large frying pan, put a medium saucepan of water on to boil and prepare a large bowl of iced water ready for the watercress.

Season the tuna steaks on both sides with salt and pepper, then fry over a very high heat for 45 seconds on each side before removing them to a plate to rest.

→

Risotto verde

WITH TUNA STEAK

(continued)

When the water has come to the boil, drop in the watercress (stalks and all) and simmer for 20 seconds before draining and immediately dunking into the ice-cold water. Let the watercress cool for 20 seconds, then drain, squeezing it in your hands to remove as much liquid as possible. Drop the watercress into a blender, add 100ml of stock and blitz until smooth.

Pour any of the remaining stock into the risotto and turn the heat back on, stirring the stock in. The risotto is ready when the rice softens, but still retains a bite. Scrape the watercress puree into the rice pan and stir to turn the whole lot a vibrant green.

Serve up the risotto on a plate topped with the tuna steaks. Sprinkle over the lemon zest and enjoy the results of your hard work.

You can make and freeze the risotto ahead if you like, then defrost, warm in the microwave, and serve with freshly cooked tuna steaks.

Aubergine caponata

WITH GRILLED MACKEREL

* Serves 2
* Make ahead

1 tbsp coconut oil

2 jarred anchovies, drained and finely chopped

1 red onion, peeled and diced

1 sprig of rosemary

2 cloves garlic, diced

250g aubergine, diced

10g tomato puree

40ml balsamic vinegar

250–350ml water

35g raisins

2 mackerel, fillets only

15g pine nuts, to serve

Melt the coconut oil in a shallow saucepan over a medium to high heat. When it is melted and hot, add the anchovies, red onion, rosemary and garlic and fry, stirring regularly, for 3 minutes.

Add the aubergine pieces and continue to stir and fry for 5 minutes.

Squeeze in the tomato puree and stir to combine. 'Cook out' the tomato puree for 1 minute – it should turn a slightly darker shade of red. Pour in the balsamic and let it bubble down to almost nothing. Pour in 250ml of water and bring to the boil. Reduce to a simmer and cook the aubergine like this for 20 minutes, or until nice and soft. Add more water to the pan if it seems it is running dry. Ultimately you're after a thick mix with most of the water being evaporated, so don't go mad pouring loads in. Stir through the raisins.

While the aubergine is cooking, heat your grill to its highest setting. Slash the mackerel fillets about three times on the skin side, then sprinkle with salt. Lay the fish, skin-side up, on a baking tray lined with baking parchment, then grill for 8 minutes without turning.

The skin on the fish should become blistered and crisp, yet perfectly cooked on the flesh side. Turn off the heat and shut the grill door to keep the fish warm.

Serve up a big plate of the caponata topped with the mackerel fillets and a sprinkling of pine nuts.

Griddled tuna

WITH SWEETCORN & LETTUCE

* Serves 2
* Barbecue

2 sweetcorn cobs
1 tbsp olive oil
2 tomatoes, sliced in half
6 spring onions, trimmed and
cut into 4cm lengths
2 × 175g tuna steaks
2 baby gem lettuces, cut in half
¼ cucumber, de-seeded and cut
into 2cm chunks
juice of 2 limes
1 red chilli, de-seeded and
finely diced
salt and black pepper
25g pumpkin seeds

Fire up the barbecue, if using. Bring a large pot of water to the boil. When the water is bubbling, carefully slide in the corn cobs and boil them for 10 minutes, then drain and pat dry with a piece of kitchen roll.

Put a griddle pan on to heat, if using. Drizzle a little oil over the corn cobs and put them onto your barbecue grill or griddle pan to cook. Slick the tomatoes and onions with oil, too, and arrange them around the corn.

The corn will take up the rest of the time to cook – they seem to take an age to colour – but turn them every now and again. The spring onions will only take about 5 minutes and the tomatoes about 6 minutes. As they cook, remove them to a bowl.

When there is space, lay on the tuna steaks in the centre of the barbecue grill or griddle pan and cook for about 1 minute on each side, then remove to a plate and leave to rest.

Drizzle the baby gem halves with olive oil and lay them on the griddle to cook. While the vegetables are cooking, mix together the cucumber pieces with the lime juice and chilli and season well with salt and pepper.

When everything is cooked, shuck the corn by standing it up on your chopping board and running your knife down the kernels, which will come off in little clumps. Add the sweetcorn to the cucumber mix.

Serve up the tomatoes and baby gem on your plate, then top with the tuna and spring onions. Spoon over the cucumber and sweetcorn relish and finish with a scattering of pumpkin seeds.

This recipe is also great with chicken or turkey steak.

Crispy sole goujons
WITH BEETROOT & APPLE

* Serves 2
* Make ahead
* Freeze ahead

50g quick-cook polenta
2 sole fillets, skinned
salt
1–2 tbsp coconut oil
4 pitta breads
1 eating apple, cheeks cut off
and sliced thinly
1 baby gem lettuce, shredded
½ red onion, finely diced
1 large, cooked beetroot, diced
(100g)
40g fat-free Greek yoghurt
1 gherkin, drained and
finely diced

Tip the polenta onto a plate. Take each sole fillet and cut it in half to make eight long, thin fillets. Season the fish all over with salt and then, one at a time, press the flesh into the polenta until the fish is well coated all over.

It is likely you'll have to cook the fish in two batches, unless you have an absolutely huge frying pan. So, in your largest non-stick frying pan, melt half of the oil over a medium to high heat, then carefully lower in four of the yellowed fillets and fry for about 2 minutes on each side. Remove to a piece of kitchen roll to blot any excess oil, then repeat the process with the remaining oil and fish.

When all the fish is cooked, put the pittas on to toast, then mix together all the remaining ingredients along with roughly ½ tablespoon of water, to loosen.

When the pittas are toasted, put them on a plate and top with the beetroot and apple salad. Place a couple of the cooked goujons on each one and serve.

Crab fu yung

* Serves 6

6 eggs
1 tbsp soy sauce
2 tsp sesame oil
½ tbsp coconut oil
4 spring onions, trimmed and finely sliced
1 fat clove garlic, finely chopped
2 pak choy, broken into leaves
200g picked white crabmeat
1 red chilli, finely sliced – remove the seeds if you don't like it hot

Beat together the eggs with the soy sauce and sesame oil and leave to one side.

Melt the coconut oil in a large non-stick frying pan over a medium to high heat, then chuck in the spring onions, garlic and pak choy and fry, tossing regularly, for 2 minutes or until the pak choy starts to wilt.

Crank up the heat to maximum and pour in the egg mix. Let it sit, bubble up and set a little. You want to try and brown the base, so leave the egg to fry for about 90 seconds, then, like an omelette, start to draw in the sides so the uncooked egg moves into the gaps.

Continue to fry and move the egg around for 2–3 minutes, or until the egg is just cooked through. Don't worry about breaking the cooked egg up. Scatter with the crabmeat, toss the mix to heat it through and serve straight up, topped with the chilli slices.

Tuna steak
WITH FRIED MUSHROOM HASH

* Serves 2

350g new potatoes, scrubbed clean and sliced in half

1 tbsp coconut oil

150g mushrooms, brushed clean and roughly cut into quarters

2 large tuna steaks

4 spring onions, trimmed and finely sliced

7 cherry tomatoes, cut in half

pinch of ground turmeric

pinch of cayenne pepper

2 handfuls of spinach leaves

MAKE IT VEG

Remove the tuna steak and replace with a couple of poached eggs.

Bring a large pot of water to the boil. When it is bubbling, drop in the potatoes and cook until tender, about 10 minutes. Drain and strain the potatoes, shaking off as much moisture as possible.

Heat up two medium frying pans over a medium to high heat and divide the oil between the two. When the oil is hot and melted, add the mushrooms to one of the pans and the tuna steaks to the other. Fry the tuna steaks for 1 minute on each side, then remove to a plate to rest.

Cook the mushrooms, without turning them too much, for 1 minute, then add the potatoes and continue to fry without stirring for a couple of minutes – you just want to colour the vegetables a little.

Add the spring onions and the cherry tomatoes to the pan and toss all together for 1 minute. Sprinkle in the turmeric and cayenne, then finish with handfuls of spinach. Turn the heat off and let the residual heat of the pan wilt the spinach.

Divide the mix over two plates, then top each mound with a tuna steak.

Salmon filo tart

* Serves 4
* Longer recipe
* Make ahead
* Freeze ahead

4 sheets of filo pastry, cut in half
40ml olive oil
1 head of broccoli, florets only
(roughly 175g) – large florets
cut in half
750g salmon fillet, skin on
80g baby spinach leaves
½ tbsp coconut oil
2 leeks, trimmed and cut into
5mm rounds
125g crème fraiche
70g cheddar, grated
1 egg, whisked
salt and black pepper
green salad, to serve

Preheat the oven to 180°C (fan 160°C/gas mark 4) and put a large pan of water on to boil.

Taking half a filo pastry sheet at a time, brush with a little olive oil and place in a deep 20cm loose-bottomed tart tin. You are aiming to totally cover the base and sides of the tin with the pastry, so arrange the pieces to cover some of the base and sides and then to hang over a little. Repeat the process with the remaining pieces of filo pastry, overlapping and arranging them to cover the tart case as completely as possible.

When you are happy with your lined tart tin, slide it into your preheated oven and bake for 12 minutes, then remove and leave to cool a little.

Meanwhile, drop your broccoli florets into the boiling water and simmer for 4 minutes before removing with a slotted spoon and cooling under cold running water.

Place the pot of water back on the hob and slide your piece(s) of fish in. Reduce the heat all the way to its lowest setting and poach the fish gently like this for 15 minutes, then remove to a plate and leave to cool a little. Put the pot of water back onto a high heat and bring to the boil.

Put the spinach into a colander, and when the water is boiling, take it off the heat and pour over the waiting spinach.

-7

Salmon filo tart

(continued)

Run cold water over the wilted spinach and when it's cold enough, pick the spinach up in your hands and give it a good squeeze to remove as much water as possible – this is important, otherwise you'll end up with a soggy tart base.

Melt the coconut oil in a pan over a medium to high heat, then drop in the sliced leeks and give them a stir. Put a lid on the pan, reduce the heat to medium to low and cook the leeks like this for 4 minutes, until softened. Turn the heat off and stir in the crème fraiche, letting it melt in the residual heat. Stir in the grated cheddar and egg and season with a little salt and pepper.

Spoon about one third of the leek sauce on the tart base, then scatter over the spinach, giving it one final squeeze before laying it in. Peel the skin off the salmon and roughly break the flesh into large chunks, and arrange most of these all over the other ingredients. Scatter over the broccoli florets, then pour over half of the remaining sauce. Scatter over the rest of the salmon, then finally pour over the rest of the sauce – it's a full tart.

Slide the tart into your oven and bake for a final 20 minutes. Take the tart out of the oven, leave to stand for 10 minutes, then remove from the tin and serve warm with a nice green salad.

PAPAYA & CASHEWS
chilli sea bass

* Serves 2

2 x 120g sea bass fillets
salt
1 bird's eye chilli, finely chopped
1 lemongrass stalk, tender white part only, finely chopped
1 garlic clove, crushed
juice of 2 limes
1 tbsp fish sauce
2 tsp sesame oil
1 large papaya, peeled, seeds removed, flesh cut into 2cm chunks
8 cherry tomatoes, roughly cut in half
large handful of bean sprouts
½ bunch of coriander, roughly chopped
½ bunch of mint, roughly chopped
¼ cucumber, de-seeded and cut into half-moons
90g toasted cashews, roughly chopped

Preheat your grill to maximum and lay the sea bass fillets skin-side up on your grill tray. Season the skin generously with salt, then slide the fish under the grill and cook for 4–5 minutes without turning. The skin should crisp up and brown and blister in places.

Turn off the heat, shut the grill door and leave the fish to keep warm.

Mix together all of the remaining ingredients, apart from the cashews.

Pile the salad high over two plates, top with the cooked fish and finish with the cashews.

Crab & sweetcorn fritters

WITH SRIRACHA MAYO

* Serves 2
* Make ahead
* Freeze ahead

200g white crabmeat

120g sweetcorn, drained

4 spring onions, trimmed and finely sliced

2 eggs

30g plain flour

salt and black pepper

1 tbsp coconut oil

50g mayonnaise

25g sriracha

juice of ½ lime

watercress, to serve

Mix together the crabmeat, sweetcorn, spring onions, eggs and flour, along with a good pinch of salt and pepper, until you reach a thick consistency.

Melt half of the oil in a large non-stick frying pan over a medium to high heat. When the oil is melted and hot, dollop in three large mounds, using up half of the mixture. Using the back of a spoon, spread the mix out to form rough circles. Fry the fritters for 3 minutes on each side, then remove to a piece of kitchen roll to drain off any excess fat. Repeat the process with the remaining oil and mixture.

Meanwhile, whisk together the mayo, sriracha and lime juice. Serve up the cakes with a large handful of watercress and a healthy dollop of hot mayo.

MAKE IT VEG

Blitz 200g cauliflower in a food processor until it resembles rice. Stir it into the mixture instead of the crabmeat and serve with chopped avocado.

PRAWN & CHICKEN
chow mein

* Serves 2

1 tbsp coconut oil

2 eggs

10 raw king prawns, peeled and cleaned

1 x 180g skinless chicken breast, cut into 1cm strips

4 spring onions, trimmed and finely sliced

3 cloves garlic, finely chopped

2 pak choy, trimmed and leaves separated

8 midget trees (tenderstem broccoli), thick stems cut in half

65g frozen peas

250g ready-to-eat egg noodles

2 tsp light soy sauce

½ tbsp kecap manis (Indonesian sweet soy sauce)

Melt a third of the oil in a large frying pan or wok over a high heat. Quickly beat the eggs together, and when the oil is melted and very hot, pour the egg in. Let the eggs puff up and fry hard for about 90 seconds. When you feel the eggs are set, flip them over and fry for a further 90 seconds – you're after a browned omelette. When cooked, tip the egg onto a piece of kitchen roll and blot off the excess oil.

Wipe the pan clean and dollop in half the remaining oil. When melted and hot, add the prawns and stir-fry for about 2 minutes or until the prawns have turned coral pink. At this point they don't have to be fully cooked through, but just coloured. Tip the prawns out and wipe out the pan.

Add the remaining oil to the pan and let it melt. When hot and melted, slide in the chicken and stir-fry for 2 minutes. Like the prawns, the chicken doesn't have to be fully cooked at this point – the idea is more to colour the meat.

Add the spring onions, garlic, pak choy, midget trees and frozen peas and stir-fry for 2 minutes. Pour in 1 tablespoon of water and let it steam through the ingredients. Add the egg noodles and stir-fry with the rest of the ingredients for 1 minute, then add the prawns back to the pan along with a second tablespoon of water. Fry the whole lot together for a minute, or until you are happy everything is fully cooked through.

Slice up the omelette into thin strips and add to the noodles. Finally, take the pan from the heat and stir through the soy sauce and kecap manis. Serve.

Cod with romesco sauce

& NEW POTATOES

* Serves 4

6 ripe tomatoes, roughly chopped

1 red onion, peeled and roughly chopped into chunks

1 red pepper, de-seeded and roughly chopped

2 red chillies, stems removed and the chillies cut in half lengthways

5 cloves garlic, left whole

drizzle of olive oil

2 slices of crusty white bread, roughly torn

800g new potatoes

½ tbsp coconut oil

4 × 200g skin-on cod fillets

salt

3 tbsp red wine vinegar

pinch of smoked paprika

basil leaves, to serve

Preheat the oven to 200°C (fan 180°C/gas mark 6).

Scatter the tomatoes, red onion, red pepper, chillies and garlic over a baking tray. Drizzle with a little olive oil, then slide into your oven and bake for 15 minutes.

Carefully remove the tray and chuck the torn-up bread on top. Return to the oven to roast for a further 10 minutes.

While the vegetables are roasting, bring a pan of water to the boil and cook the new potatoes for about 15 minutes or until just tender. Drain and keep to one side.

At the same time as the potatoes are boiling, melt the coconut oil in a large ovenproof frying pan over a medium to high heat. Season the skin side of the cod with salt, then gently lay the fish in the pan, skin-side down. Fry the fish without flipping for 4 minutes, then flip over and put the whole frying pan in the oven for 5 minutes, by which time the fish should be just cooked through.

When the vegetables have had their time in the oven, remove them and carefully transfer them, plus any juices in the pan, to a food processor. Add the red wine vinegar and paprika along with a good pinch of salt and pepper and blitz until almost smooth.

Serve up the cod and potatoes with the sauce and a scattering of basil leaves.

Spice-roasted salmon

WITH PANEER & CAULIFLOWER

* Serves 2

½ tbsp coconut oil

1 small head of cauliflower broken into small florets (360g)

½ courgette, cut into half-moons (about 130g)

1 small red onion, peeled and cut into thin wedges

1½ tsp curry powder

salt and black pepper

50g kale, thick stalks removed

125g paneer, cut into 2cm cubes

1 green chilli, cut into thin rounds

2 × 200g salmon fillets, skin on

small bunch of coriander, roughly chopped

2 tbsp Greek yoghurt

1 lemon, cut into wedges, to serve

Preheat the oven to 200°C (fan 180°C/gas mark 6). Dollop the coconut oil onto a baking tray and slide into the oven to preheat for 5 minutes.

Toss the cauliflower, courgette and red onion in a bowl with 1 teaspoon of the curry powder and a little salt and pepper. Carefully remove the hot tray from the oven and transfer the spiced vegetables onto the tray and slide back into the oven to roast for 10 minutes.

While the vegetables are roasting, toss the kale, paneer and green chilli with the remaining curry powder and another pinch of salt and pepper. Season the salmon on its skin side.

Take the tray from the oven and give the cauliflower and other vegetables a turn. Scatter them with the spiced paneer, kale and chilli, then lay the seasoned salmon fillets on top, salt-side up.

Slide the tray back into the oven and cook for a final 15 minutes.

Remove the tray and sprinkle with chopped coriander. Add a dollop of yoghurt and a wedge of lemon and serve up.

Pork

GRIDDLED
peach & asparagus
WITH BURRATA

* Serves 2
* Barbecue

1½ tbsp olive oil

2 peaches, stoned and cut into quarters

100g asparagus

2 burrata, drained

4 slices of parma ham

2 handfuls of rocket

20g toasted, flaked almonds

a little drizzle of balsamic vinegar

Fire up the barbecue or heat a large griddle pan over a high heat.

Drizzle a little of the olive oil all over the peaches and asparagus and give them a good smoosh around, so they are covered all over with the oil.

Place the peaches and asparagus on the outer, slightly cooler edges of the barbecue and cook for about 5 minutes. Turn the asparagus regularly. If the peaches are ripe, they will need less time. You are looking just to caramelize the peach flesh and to take any hard bite away – there is no hard and fast rule to this. Barbecue the asparagus until lightly charred and just tender.

If you are cooking on the griddle pan, cook the peaches first, then remove the pieces to a plate and cook the asparagus for about 4 minutes, turning regularly until lightly charred.

Lay the burrata and parma ham on a plate and then build up the salad using the rocket, griddled peaches and asparagus, and finish with a scattering of toasted almonds and a drizzle of balsamic vinegar.

Photo on previous page

Manchego saltimbocca
WITH PEAR & ROCKET SALAD

* Serves 4
* Freeze ahead

4 × 175g thin pork escalopes
(roughly 18 × 12cm in size)

24 sage leaves, finely chopped

8 slices of manchego cheese,
plus a little extra for the salad,
rind removed

16 slices of parma ham

1 tbsp coconut oil

1 pear, sliced thinly

4 handfuls of rocket

40g pecan nuts,
roughly chopped

drizzle of balsamic vinegar

Take each piece of pork in turn and cut it in half widthways. Sprinkle chopped sage over both sides of the meat, then crumble a small slice of manchego onto one side of the meat.

Draw the meat over the cheese to envelop it, then wrap the small parcel in two slices of parma ham. Repeat the process with all of the remaining slices of pork and cheese until you are left with eight little wrapped parcels.

Melt half of the oil in a large non-stick frying pan over a medium to high heat, then fry four of the parcels for about 3 minutes on each side. Remove and keep warm while you repeat the process with the remaining parcels.

When you have cooked all of your saltimbocca, make a salad by tossing together the thinly sliced pear with the rocket and then shaving off fine slices of cheese with a potato peeler.

Plate up the perfect parcels with a big handful of salad, a sprinkling of chopped pecan nuts and a drizzle of balsamic.

Grilled pork chops

WITH APPLE & DILL COLESLAW

* Serves 4
* Barbecue

4 large pork chops, fat removed
if you prefer

1 carrot, peeled and julienned
(140g)

1 large apple, julienned (100g)

3 sticks of celery, trimmed and
finely sliced on the angle (100g)

1 red onion, peeled and finely
sliced

¼ small white cabbage (200g)

85g mayonnaise

1 tbsp white wine vinegar

small bunch of dill, finely
chopped

2 tsp dijon mustard

watercress, to serve

Fire up the barbecue or preheat your grill to maximum.

Lay your chops on the barbecue or grill tray (if possible, cover
the barbecue to ensure even cooking). Cook for 6–7 minutes,
then turn the chops over and cook for a further 6–7 minutes,
or until you are happy the meat is cooked through – you can
check this by cutting into a thick part of the meat and ensuring
the flesh has turned white.

If you're cooking under the grill, turn the heat off, shut the grill
door and leave the meat to rest until you're ready to serve.
Otherwise cover with foil.

While the chops are cooking, toss together the carrot, apple,
celery, red onion and cabbage. Add the mayo, vinegar, dill
and mustard and mix the whole lot together until the vegetables
are evenly coated in the mayo mix.

Serve up the chops with a good heap of coleslaw and a handful
of watercress.

*Take the meat out of the fridge 15 minutes before cooking it –
it ensures you can cook the meat all the way through without
it drying out.*

Summer salad
WITH COURGETTE & HAM

* Serves 2

3 eggs
75g gherkins, drained and finely chopped
30g capers, drained and roughly chopped
40ml olive oil
small bunch of dill, finely chopped
small bunch of chives, finely chopped
1 medium courgette
75g fresh peas
300g thick-cut, deli-style ham
30g walnuts, roughly chopped

Cook the eggs in a pan of boiling water for 8 minutes, then drain and cool under cold running water. Peel and leave to one side.

Mix together the gherkins, capers, olive oil, dill and chives in a large bowl.

Take your courgette and, using a peeler, create long thin ribbons along the entire length of the courgette. When you get close to the core, rotate the courgette and continue on the other side. You won't be able to make ribbons with the whole courgette, so just keep what's left of the core for another recipe, such as a stir-fry.

Add the courgette ribbons to the bowl of dressing along with the peas and toss the whole lot together.

Slice the boiled eggs into rounds. Build up your courgette salad on two plates, tearing the ham into it and laying on the egg slices. Finish with some chopped walnuts and get stuck in.

MAKE IT VEG
Omit the ham and replace with 1 chopped avocado and a generous sprinkling of flaxseeds.

PORK & KIDNEY BEAN
burritos

* Serves 4

600g pork tenderloin, trimmed of visible fat

1½ tsp sweet smoked paprika

½ tsp cayenne pepper – add more or less, depending on your resilience

1½ tsp ground cumin

1 red onion, finely sliced

4 cloves garlic, minced

large bunch of coriander

salt and black pepper

½ tbsp coconut oil

1 x 400g tin of chopped tomatoes

180g kidney beans (drained weight)

200g pre-cooked rice

4 large tortilla wraps

1 iceberg lettuce, shredded, to serve

Cut the pork into large 4cm chunks, then put them in a bowl and add the paprika, cayenne, cumin, onion, garlic and the finely chopped stalks of the coriander. Add a pinch of salt and pepper and give the whole lot a good stir and leave to sit for 5 minutes.

After 5 minutes, melt the coconut oil in a large frying pan over a high heat, and when the oil is hot and melted, tip the entire contents of the bowl into the pan. Fry the mix for about 5 minutes, but only stirring occasionally – you're after a bit of colour on the pork and onions if possible.

When everything in the pan is a little wilted down, pour in the chopped tomatoes and kidney beans along with a little splash of water. Bring the whole lot to the boil, then simmer for 5 minutes or until you are happy the pork is fully cooked through – you can check this by cutting into a thick piece and ensuring it has turned from fleshy pink to cooked white.

Chop up the remaining coriander leaves and stir through. Heat up the tortilla wraps – I do this in the microwave – and serve up.

Spoon some of the rice onto the wraps, add the pork and beans and finish with a good handful of shredded iceberg lettuce. Wrap up and serve up.

* I like using pre-cooked rice, but if you prefer you could cook 70g rice according to packet instructions.

Chickpea & veg stew

WITH PORK TENDERLOIN

* Serves 4

1 tbsp coconut oil
1 red onion, peeled and sliced
½ courgette, grated
1 small carrot, peeled and grated
3 cloves garlic, roughly chopped
1 red chilli, finely sliced – remove the seeds if you don't like it hot
½ tsp ground cumin
½ tsp ground coriander
¼ tsp cayenne pepper
salt and black pepper
300g fresh tomatoes, roughly chopped
1 × 400g tin of chickpeas, drained
65g prunes, roughly chopped
750g piece of pork tenderloin
small bunch of coriander, roughly chopped
crusty bread, to serve

Heat half of the coconut oil in a large frying pan over a medium to high heat, then add the red onion and fry for 2 minutes, stirring regularly.

Add the courgette, carrot, garlic and chilli and crank up the heat to maximum. Fry the ingredients, stirring regularly, for about 2 minutes, by which time they should be breaking down.

Reduce the heat and sprinkle in the cumin, coriander, cayenne pepper and a good pinch of both salt and pepper.

Add the tomatoes, chickpeas and prunes, along with a splash of water. As the tomatoes cook, they will break down and release liquid. However, if you feel the pan is cooking dry, then add a small splash of water. Leave the mix to cook for 10 minutes.

In the meantime, take the pork tenderloin and cut into four roughly equal cylinders, trimming off any large pieces of fat and sinew. Take each loin cylinder and slice down the length, making sure you don't cut all the way through the meat. Open the meat like a book and give it a couple of pushes with the palm of your hand. Repeat the process with the remaining pieces of meat and then season well with salt and pepper.

Melt the remaining oil in a large frying pan over a medium to high heat. When the oil is melted and hot, lay the pork tenderloins in and cook for 10 minutes, turning regularly. Remove the pork to a plate and leave to rest for 5 minutes.

Serve up the stew, slice up the tenderloin and lay it on top. Finish with coriander and wolf down with a thick slice of bread.

Harissa pork chops

WITH FENNEL & PARSLEY SALAD

* Serves 2
* Barbecue

2 large pork chops
1 heaped tablespoon of rose harissa paste
salt
8 pitted green olives, cut in half
20g preserved lemon, roughly cut into small pieces
30g walnuts, roughly chopped
40g feta, roughly crumbled
1 large fennel bulb, trimmed and finely sliced
small bunch of parsley, roughly chopped
25ml olive oil

Fire up the barbecue or turn your grill on to maximum.

Lay your pork chops on a plate and spoon on the harissa paste. Using your hands or a spoon, smother the meat with the red paste. Give them a little sprinkle of salt.

Lay your chops on the barbecue or grill tray (if possible, cover the barbecue to ensure even cooking). Cook for 6–7 minutes, then turn the chops over and cook for a further 6–7 minutes, or until you are happy the meat is cooked through – you can check this by cutting into a thick part of the meat and ensuring the flesh has turned white.

If you're cooking under the grill, turn the heat off, shut the grill door and leave the meat to rest until you're ready to serve. Otherwise cover with foil.

While the chops are cooking, place all of the remaining ingredients into a bowl and toss together.

Serve up the salad topped with a spicy pork chop.

If you don't like pork chops, try this with lamb chops or chicken thighs.

Sausage & mushroom pie

* Serves 4
* Longer recipe
* Freeze ahead

½ tbsp coconut oil

12 sausages

2 large onions, peeled and finely sliced

2 carrots, peeled and diced

2 sticks of celery, trimmed and diced

5 sprigs of thyme

1 bay leaf

250g chestnut mushrooms, brushed clean and roughly chopped into quarters

salt and black pepper

200ml chicken stock

200ml ale (I use London Pride)

30ml Worcestershire sauce

10g cornflour

3 large sheets of filo pastry

1 tbsp olive oil

2 tsp nigella seeds

buttered greens, to serve

Melt the oil in a large, high-sided frying pan over a medium to high heat, then roll the sausages into the pan and brown all over. Don't worry about cooking the sausages through at this point – all you want is for them to go dark brown. Remove the sausages from the pan and then add the onions.

Cook the onions for about 8 minutes, or until softened and caramelized. Add the carrots, celery, thyme and bay leaf and cook for a further 2 minutes, stirring frequently over a high heat.

Add the chestnut mushrooms along with a good pinch of both salt and pepper, and continue to stir-fry for another couple of minutes, then add the stock, ale and Worcestershire sauce. Bring the liquid slowly up to the boil (rapid boiling makes it taste bitter), then reduce to a simmer and cook for 10 minutes.

Mix the cornflour with just enough water to make it into a liquid, then pour into the mix and stir to thicken.

Tip the mix into a 29 x 20cm baking dish and preheat the oven to 190°C (fan 170°C/gas mark 5). Let the mix cool just a little in the baking dish, then take the sheets of filo, scrunch a little and cover the filling. Brush randomly with olive oil and sprinkle with the nigella seeds.

Slide the dish into the oven and bake for 20–25 minutes, by which time the pastry will be crisp and coloured on top and cooked through underneath. Serve up with steaming buttered greens.

ROAST CHICORY AND PECANS
with salami

* Serves 2

4 chicory heads – I like to use
2 red and 2 yellow

2 tbsp olive oil

½ red onion, peeled and
finely sliced

juice of ½ orange

½ tbsp red wine vinegar

½ fennel bulb, trimmed and
finely sliced

16 slices of best-quality salami

30g pecans, roughly chopped

Preheat the oven to 190°C (fan 170°C/gas mark 5).

Cut the chicory heads in half lengthways, discarding any of the brown outer leaves. Lay the chicory on a roasting tray, cut-side up, and drizzle with a little olive oil. Roast in the oven for 25 minutes until lightly caramelized and tender, but still holding their shape.

Meanwhile, drop the sliced red onion into a bowl and pour over the orange juice and red wine vinegar. Leave the onions to macerate while the chicory heads are cooking.

When the chicory heads have had their time in the oven, divide them between the two plates. Spoon some of the macerated onions over the chicory, reserving the soaking juices.

Pile up the fennel, salami and pecans and finally finish with spoonfuls of the soaking juices.

Beef &
Lamb

KOFTA-STUFFED
Romano peppers

* Serves 4

4 large Romano peppers, halved lengthways, seeds removed

10ml olive oil

1 tbsp coconut oil

2 red onions, peeled and finely sliced

3 cloves garlic, finely chopped

1 aubergine, trimmed and diced into 1cm cubes (250g)

250g lamb mince

250g beef mince

½ tsp ground cinnamon

1 tsp ground cumin

½ tsp sweet smoked paprika

salt and black pepper

1 tbsp tomato puree

100ml beef stock

70g pine nuts

½ bunch of coriander, roughly chopped

225g pizza mozzarella, patted dry

rocket, to serve

Preheat the oven to 210°C (fan 190°C/gas mark 6–7).

Lay the peppers on a baking tray in a single layer, drizzle over the olive oil and roast in the hot oven for 20 minutes.

Meanwhile, melt the coconut oil in a large frying pan over a medium to high heat, then add the red onion and garlic and fry for 3–4 minutes or until just soft.

Crank up the heat to maximum and add the aubergine and both types of mince. Fry the ingredients over the high heat, stirring occasionally for a few minutes, breaking up the mince with a wooden spoon. Sprinkle in the cinnamon, cumin and paprika and stir to incorporate.

Season with a generous amount of salt and pepper, then add the tomato puree along with the beef stock and let the mixture simmer away – you don't want it to be too wet. After a couple of minutes, turn the heat off and stir through the pine nuts and chopped coriander.

Remove the roasted peppers from the oven. They should have collapsed a little but still be holding their shape. Carefully drain off liquid that may have been produced while roasting, then fill the cavities with the mixture. Don't worry if the mixture falls over the side.

Slice or tear the mozzarella and arrange over the top of the mince, then slide the tray back into the oven and bake for a further 10 minutes. The mozzarella will have melted nicely by this point. Serve up with a generous helping of rocket.

Spiced lamb chops

WITH CUCUMBER SALAD

* Serves 4
* Barbecue

2 tsp ground cumin
3 tsp sea salt
12 lamb loin chops
100g Greek yoghurt
bunch of dill, roughly chopped
juice of ½ lemon
½ cucumber, de-seeded and cut
into chunks
12 cherry tomatoes, cut in half
½ red onion, peeled and diced
2 tbsp balsamic vinegar
salt and black pepper
60g toasted pine nuts

Fire up the barbecue or preheat your grill to maximum. Mix together the cumin and salt and season your lamb chops all over with the spiced salt.

Lay your chops on the outer, slightly cooler edges of the barbecue, or grill tray (if possible, cover the barbecue to ensure even cooking). Cook for 5–6 minutes, then turn the chops over and cook for a further 5–6 minutes, or until you are happy the meat is cooked through.

If you're cooking under the grill, turn the heat off, shut the grill door and leave the meat to rest until you're ready to serve (at least 5 minutes). Otherwise cover with foil.

Tip the yoghurt into a bowl and mix it with three-quarters of the dill and the lemon juice.

Mix together the cucumber, cherry tomatoes, red onion and balsamic vinegar, seasoning with a little salt and pepper.

Serve up the spiced lamb chops, with the salad, yoghurt and a scattering of the reserved dill and the pine nuts.

Paprika lamb kebabs

WITH WHIPPED HERB RICOTTA

* Serves 4
* Barbecue

drizzle of olive oil

½ tsp ground cumin

½ tsp sweet smoked paprika

salt and black pepper

700g lamb steak, cut into 3cm chunks, hard fat removed (if any)

350g ricotta

2 tbsp extra virgin olive oil

small bunch of chives, finely chopped

½ bunch of parsley, finely chopped

juice of ½ lemon

3 cooked beetroot, drained and cut into large chunks

4 handfuls of rocket

40g walnuts, roughly chopped

Fire up the barbecue or put a heavy-based griddle pan on to heat over a medium to high flame.

Mix together the oil, cumin and paprika along with a big pinch of salt and pepper. Thread the meat onto four long skewers – you want the meat to touch, but don't squash it on otherwise it won't cook at all.

Swoosh the skewered meat through the spice mix, trying to ensure a thin, even layer all over. Lay the kebabs on the outer, slightly cooler part of the barbecue, or the hot griddle pan and fry, turning every 2–3 minutes for about 10 minutes, or until the meat is lovely and browned on the outside and just cooked through on the inside. Remove the meat to rest for at least 5 minutes.

While the meat is resting, tip the ricotta into a bowl and add the extra virgin olive oil along with a good pinch of salt. Whip the ricotta with a whisk for about 30 seconds or until it is totally smooth. Stir through the chopped chives, parsley and lemon juice and then divide over four plates. Place a lamb skewer onto each plate, then divide out the beetroot, rocket and walnuts.

AVOCADO & GOAT'S CHEESE WITH
grilled lamb chops

* Serves 2

6 lamb loin chops
salt and black pepper
10 cherry tomatoes
1 large avocado, de-stoned
70g soft goat's cheese
60g Greek yoghurt
30ml olive oil
small bunch of chives,
finely sliced
½ small bunch of mint,
finely chopped
rocket, to serve

Turn on your grill to maximum. Lay the lamb chops on your grill tray and season with a little salt and pepper. Cook the chops under the grill for 8 minutes, then flip them, scatter the cherry tomatoes on the same tray and cook for a further 4–5 minutes. Shut the grill door, turn off the heat and leave the chops to rest.

While the lamb is resting, place the avocado flesh, goat's cheese, yoghurt and olive oil into a food processor and blitz until smooth. Remove to a bowl and stir in the chives and mint along with a little salt and pepper.

Serve up the chops with a big dollop of the avocado tzatziki, the cherry tomatoes and a big handful of rocket.

Quick spiced beef

* Serves 4

½ tbsp coconut oil

1 red onion, peeled and diced

1 aubergine, trimmed and cut into 1cm dice

1 red pepper, de-seeded and cut into 1cm dice

3 cloves garlic, finely chopped

600g beef mince

½ tsp ground cinnamon

½ tsp ground cumin

1 tbsp flour

200ml beef stock

40g raisins

To serve

500g pre-cooked rice

shredded lettuce

small bunch of coriander, roughly chopped

Melt the coconut oil in a large frying pan over a medium to high heat, then add the red onion and cook for 2 minutes. Chuck in the aubergine, red pepper and chopped garlic. Fry the ingredients for 5 minutes.

Crank up the heat to maximum and push the vegetables to one side. Plonk the meat straight into the frying pan and fry without moving it for 1 minute, then get stuck in and break the meat up. Keep frying and breaking up the meat for a couple of minutes or until it is well broken up.

Add the ground spices and flour and mix to make sure there are no lumps, then pour in the stock and add the raisins. Bring the liquid to the boil and simmer for 5 minutes.

Serve up the spiced beef on rice with a side of shredded lettuce and a sprinkling of chopped coriander.

I like using pre-cooked rice, but if you prefer you could cook 170g rice according to packet instructions.

Grilled sirloin wraps
WITH WASABI DRESSING

* Serves 2

2 cloves garlic, minced

3cm ginger, peeled and minced

1 tbsp soy sauce

1 tbsp honey

2 sirloin steaks, visible fat removed

200g pre-cooked rice

½ tbsp wasabi

1½ tbsp rice wine vinegar

1 tsp sesame oil

2 plain tortilla wraps

4 radishes, thinly sliced

2 spring onions, trimmed and finely sliced

shredded iceberg lettuce, to serve

Mix together the garlic, ginger, soy sauce and honey until combined. Lay the steaks in the mixture, swishing them about a bit to make sure they're evenly coated, then leave the steaks to sit for 10 minutes.

Heat a griddle pan over maximum heat. When the steaks have had their 10 minutes, take them from the bowl, scraping off any excess marinade, and lay the meat gently in the griddle pan. Fry, turning regularly, for 4 minutes on each side. Remove the steaks to a plate to rest.

While the steaks are resting, ping the rice in the microwave, then whisk together the wasabi, vinegar and sesame oil. Warm through the tortillas in either the microwave or a dry frying pan.

Lay out the tortillas, then divide the rice over the middle of each one. Slice the steak, then place it on top of the rice and drizzle the wasabi dressing over the cooked meat. Pile up the radishes, spring onions and lettuce, then wrap the tortillas as well as you can and chow down.

* Make sure you cook the steaks from room temperature, otherwise you may burn them on the outside and leave them raw in the middle. I like using pre-cooked rice, but if you prefer you could cook 70g rice according to packet instructions.

SWEDISH-STYLE
meatballs

* Serves 2

450ml double cream
2 cloves garlic, minced
2 bay leaves
½ tbsp coconut oil
800g small ready-made
meatballs (or see Tip below)
20g gruyère or mature
cheddar, grated
75g pomegranate seeds –
optional

To serve
large bunch of dill, leaves only
steamed greens

Pour the cream into a wide saucepan, add the garlic and bay leaves and bring to a low simmer, stirring frequently. Let the cream simmer for 5 minutes to reduce by a third.

While the cream is reducing, melt half of the coconut oil in a large frying pan over a medium to high heat. When the oil is melted and hot, roll half of the meatballs in and brown all over. The meatballs should be virtually cooked by the time they are browned. Remove the balls to a plate with a slotted spoon, wipe out the pan with some kitchen roll and repeat the process with the remaining oil and balls.

Reduce the heat under the cream and stir in the grated cheese until it has melted and is fully incorporated. Tip the balls, along with any residual cooking liquids, into the cheese and gently stir to coat. Serve up the meatballs scattered with pomegranate seeds, if using, and dill, alongside some steamed greens.

To make your own meatballs, mix together 750g beef mince, 35g fresh breadcrumbs and 1 egg in a bowl using your hands. Season with salt and pepper and shape into roughly 20 little balls. Continue with the recipe.

Roast pepper gnocchi
WITH SIRLOIN STEAK

* Serves 4

1 tbsp coconut oil

1 red onion, peeled and finely sliced

small bunch of basil (20g), roughly chopped

100g jarred red pepper, drained and cut into 1cm strips

2 x 200g sirloin steaks, visible fat removed

300g ready-to-cook fresh gnocchi

balsamic glaze dressing, to finish

Melt half of the oil in a large frying pan over a medium heat, and at the same time put a large saucepan of water on to boil. As soon as the oil has melted and is hot, add the onion and fry gently, stirring regularly for about 8 minutes or until the onions are very soft.

Put a second pan on over a high heat for the steaks.

Add half of the chopped basil to the onions, along with the roasted red pepper, and stir everything together. As soon as the peppers are warmed through, turn the heat off under the pan.

Add the remaining coconut oil to the pan over the high heat, then lay in the steaks. Cook the steaks according to preference – I like my steak medium rare, so 2½ minutes on each side, turning regularly – then leave to rest until you're ready to eat.

While the steak is resting, carefully drop the gnocchi into the boiling water and simmer according to packet instructions (normally about 3 minutes). You know they're done when they float to the surface.

->

Roast pepper gnocchi

WITH SIRLOIN STEAK

(continued)

Before draining off the gnocchi, save about a quarter of a mugful of the cooking water and add to the pan with the sweated onions and peppers. Drain the gnocchi and add to the onion pan.

Turn the heat back on under the onions, which now have the gnocchi in as well, and gently stir the whole lot together until the gnocchi are nicely covered with the sauce and everything is heated through.

Stir through the remaining basil, leaving a little for garnish if you like, then serve up on two plates. Slice the steak and serve on top of the gnocchi, all finished with a tasty drizzle of balsamic glaze.

Sumac lamb chops
WITH ROAST LETTUCE

* Serves 2

1 clove garlic, grated
1½ tbsp olive oil
2 baby gem lettuces
10 cherry tomatoes
6 lamb chops
salt and black pepper
2 tsp sumac
65g Greek yoghurt
25g tahini
juice of ½ lemon
40g pomegranate seeds
½ small bunch of mint,
leaves only

Preheat the oven to 210°C (fan 190°C/gas mark 6–7) and turn your grill up to maximum.

Mix together the grated garlic and olive oil in a small bowl.

Cut the baby gem lettuces in half lengthways and lay on a roasting tray. Place the tomatoes close by, then spoon about two-thirds of the garlic and oil over the cut side of the lettuces and the tomatoes. Slide the tray into the oven and roast for 12 minutes.

Lay the lamb chops down and season with salt and pepper, then sprinkle over the sumac and rub to ensure an even coating. Cook the lamb chops under the hot grill for 7 minutes, then flip and cook for a further 4 minutes on the other side. When they are cooked, turn the heat off and shut the grill door to keep them warm until you're ready to eat.

Mix together the remaining garlic oil, yoghurt, tahini and lemon juice in a small bowl along with about 75ml of water to make a fairly runny sauce.

Plate up the roasted lettuce topped with the tomatoes and the spiced lamb chops and finish with the garlicky sauce, pomegranate seeds and mint leaves.

* You could also use the slightly cheaper lamb-leg steaks for this recipe.

Fennel & lemon lamb chops

WITH BUTTERY PEAS

* Serves 2

6 lamb loin chops
1½ tsp fennel seeds
1 lemon
salt and black pepper
300g frozen peas
30g butter
1 red chilli, de-seeded and finely chopped
3 spring onions, trimmed and finely sliced
½ bunch of mint, leaves roughly chopped
watercress, to serve

Crank up your grill to maximum and lay the lamb chops on your grill tray.

Using a pestle and mortar, smash up the fennel seeds – not to a dust, but they should become pretty small. (If you don't have a pestle and mortar, just lay the seeds on your board and chop through them a few times.) Sprinkle the fennel seeds all over the lamb chops, then grate lemon zest over them, too. Season with salt and pepper, then grill for 8 minutes before turning and grilling for a further 6 minutes. Turn off the heat, shut the grill door and leave the lamb to rest.

While the lamb is cooking, put a pot of water on to boil. When the water is bubbling away, add the peas and cook for about 6 minutes – you are looking to slightly overcook the peas. Drain the peas and leave to one side.

Add the butter to the still-warm saucepan and melt over a medium heat. Chuck in the red chilli and spring onions and fry for 2 minutes. Tumble the peas back in and give the whole lot a good toss.

Turn the heat off under the peas and use a potato masher to rough them up – you're not trying to mash them all, more just crush them.

Serve up the peas topped with the lamb chops, mint leaves, a handful of watercress and the zested lemon, wedged.

Lamb-leg steaks are a lovely cheaper option.

Sirloin steaks
WITH GARLICKY CREAMY SPINACH

* Serves 2

20g butter
2 cloves garlic, finely chopped
450g frozen spinach
½ tbsp coconut oil
2 sirloin steaks
100ml double cream
50g parmesan
grating of nutmeg

Melt the butter in a medium frying pan over a medium to high heat, then add the chopped garlic and fry for 1 minute. Add the frozen spinach to the pan and reduce the heat to medium. For the next 5 minutes, warm the spinach through in the pan, giving it the occasional prod to break the large lumps up.

While the spinach is defrosting, melt the coconut oil in a second frying pan over a high heat. When the oil is hot and melted, cook the steaks according to preference – I like my steaks medium rare, so 2½ minutes on each side, turning regularly – then leave to rest until you're ready to eat.

As the spinach defrosts it will release a lot of water. Without destroying the spinach, drain off as much as you can, then stir in the double cream and bring to a light boil. Turn the heat off underneath, and stir through the parmesan and grated nutmeg.

Divide the spinach over two plates, then top with the perfectly cooked steaks.

SIRLOIN STEAK WITH
chimichurri

* Serves 2

2 tbsp olive oil

1 banana shallot, peeled and diced

1 tsp thyme leaves

3g oregano leaves, roughly chopped

7g parsley leaves, roughly chopped

150g cherry tomatoes, cut in half

salt and pepper

2 tsp balsamic vinegar

½ tbsp coconut oil

2 sirloin steaks

grilled or steamed midget trees (tenderstem broccoli), to serve

Pour the olive oil into a medium saucepan over a medium to low heat. Add the shallot, thyme, oregano, parsley and cherry tomatoes and leave to 'cook' very gently, stirring every now and then for 15 minutes, by which time all the ingredients will have released their flavours. Turn the heat off, sprinkle in a good amount of salt and pepper along with the balsamic and stir.

While the sauce is cooking, melt the coconut oil in a frying pan over a high heat. Lay in the steaks and cook according to preference – I like my steak medium rare, so 2½ minutes on each side, turning regularly – then leave to rest until you're ready to eat.

Serve up the steak with a generous helping of midget trees, all topped with the tasty sauce.

Beef & lemongrass
NOODLE SOUP

* Serves 2

1 tbsp coconut oil

2 lemongrass stalks, tender white part only, finely sliced

1 stick of celery, finely chopped

1 star anise

1 stick of cinnamon

4cm ginger, peeled and roughly chopped

1 bird's eye chilli, split lengthways

juice and zest of 1 lime

4 spring onions, trimmed and finely sliced

2 tomatoes, roughly chopped

600ml chicken stock

2 sirloin steaks

300g ready-to-eat rice noodles

1 tbsp fish sauce

fresh coriander, to serve

Melt half of the coconut oil in a saucepan over a medium to high heat, then add the lemongrass, celery, star anise, cinnamon stick, ginger, chilli, lime zest and two of the sliced spring onions. Let the ingredients fry for a couple of minutes, then add the chopped-up tomatoes and fry until the tomatoes begin to break down.

Pour in the chicken stock and bring the whole lot to the boil, then reduce to a low simmer and cook for 10 minutes.

While the soup is simmering away, melt the remaining oil in a large frying pan over a high heat, then gently lay the steaks in the pan. Fry the steaks for 4 minutes on each side, turning regularly. When the steaks have had their cooking time, remove them to a plate to rest.

Bring a kettle to the boil and tip the noodles into a sieve. When the kettle has boiled, pour the water over the noodles. Give the noodles a shake to remove the excess liquid, then divide between two deep bowls.

Sieve the simmered soup broth into a jug and stir in the fish sauce and the juice of the lime. Pour the broth over the noodles, then slice up the steak and lay it on top of the noodles. Finish with a scattering of coriander and the remaining two finely sliced spring onions.

Drink up and feel yourself being restored.

Beef-stuffed aubergine

WITH HALLOUMI & GREEN OLIVES

* Serves 2

2 aubergines
drizzle of olive oil
½ tbsp coconut oil
1 red onion, peeled and diced
2 cloves garlic, finely chopped
½ tsp fenugreek seeds
½ tsp ground turmeric
½ tsp chilli powder
½ tsp ground coriander
400g beef mince
100g mushrooms, brushed
clean and roughly chopped
into small pieces
1 beef stock cube
salt and black pepper
40g pitted green olives, drained
and roughly chopped
100g halloumi, grated
rocket, to serve
drizzle of balsamic vinegar

Preheat the oven to 200°C (fan 180°C/gas mark 6).

Take each aubergine one at a time and cut in half lengthways. Score the flesh, making sure not to cut all the way through the skin. Using a spoon, scratch out the aubergine flesh, leaving only a thin flesh border attached to the skin. Lay the hulled-out aubergine halves on a baking tray, drizzle with olive oil and roast in the oven for 15 minutes.

While the aubergine is baking, melt the coconut oil in a frying pan over a medium to high heat, then add the red onion, garlic and fenugreek seeds and fry, stirring regularly, for 5 minutes.

Sprinkle in the rest of the spices and stir to combine. Crank up the heat to maximum and add the beef mince. Leave it without prodding for 2 minutes to try and brown a little. Add the mushrooms to the pan and stir together. Cut the aubergine flesh (about 200g) into small pieces, then add this to the pan, too.

Crumble the stock cube and stir in, along with a good pinch of salt and pepper. Put a lid on the pan and leave to cook for 10 minutes.

Turn off the heat, remove the lid and stir through the green olives. The aubergines will have cooked by now, so carefully remove them and then fill the cavity with the beef mixture. Sprinkle over the halloumi, then slide the halves back into the oven for a final 5–10 minutes.

Serve up with a big handful of rocket and a drizzling of balsamic.

OLIVE, ARTICHOKE, QUINOA &
steak salad

* Serves 2

½ tbsp coconut oil

2 sirloin steaks, any visible fat removed

350g pre-cooked quinoa – red and white mixed

175g jarred artichokes, thoroughly drained and roughly chopped

100g pitted green olives, drained and roughly chopped

1 preserved lemon, peel only, finely chopped

large bunch of parsley, roughly chopped

2 small handfuls of rocket, to serve

Melt the coconut oil in a large frying pan over a high heat, then gently lay the steaks in it and fry for 4 minutes on each side, turning regularly. Remove the steaks to a plate to rest.

Zap the quinoa in a microwave according to the packet instructions. When hot, carefully tip into a large bowl and add the artichokes, olives, preserved lemon peel and parsley. Give the whole lot a good stir and then divide over two plates.

Slice the steak into thick chunks and top the quinoa with it. Finish with a little handful of rocket.

STEAK WITH KALE, TAHINI &
sesame greens

* Serves 2

1 tbsp coconut oil

2 cloves garlic, finely chopped

200g kale, thick stalks removed

½ courgette, trimmed and cut into half-moons

125g midget trees (tenderstem broccoli), thick stalks cut in half lengthways

150ml hot chicken stock

2 sirloin steaks

salt

30g tahini

3 tsp sesame oil

2 red chillies, de-seeded and finely chopped

sesame seeds, to serve

Melt half of the coconut oil in a large frying pan over a medium to high heat, then add the chopped garlic and cook for 30 seconds. Add the kale, courgette and midget trees and fry, stirring regularly, for 3 minutes.

Pour the hot stock into the pan with the greens. Reduce the heat to medium and cook for 5 minutes, stirring every now and again.

In the meantime, heat the remaining oil in a frying pan over a high heat, and gently lay in the steaks. Cook the steaks for 4 minutes on each side, turning them regularly as they cook. Remove the steaks to a plate to rest and season them with salt.

Check the vegetables are just tender, then take the pan off the heat. Mix the tahini with the sesame oil in a small bowl.

Serve up the greens topped with the sliced steak, red chilli, sesame seeds and a drizzle of the sesame and tahini dressing.

One-pan steak
WITH DEVILLED MUSHROOMS

* Serves 2

¾ tbsp coconut oil

1 red onion, peeled and diced

8 chestnut mushrooms, brushed clean and roughly cut in half

3 sprigs of thyme

350g fillet steak, cut into 3cm chunks

¾ tsp sweet smoked paprika

pinch of cayenne pepper

salt and black pepper

200g crème fraiche

1½ tsp dijon mustard

2 large handfuls of baby spinach leaves

juice of ½ lemon

steamed green beans, to serve

Melt half of the coconut oil in a large frying pan over a medium to high heat. then add the diced onion and fry for 3–4 minutes, stirring regularly.

Crank up the heat to maximum and toss in the chopped mushrooms and thyme sprigs. Fry the ingredients all together, stirring every now and again – the aim is to soften the vegetables, but also to catch a little colour without burning.

Transfer the onions and mushrooms to a plate. Melt the remaining coconut oil in the pan, then add the steak and fry hard, turning only now and again. You want to colour the meat – the cooking will take care of itself.

Once the meat is well coloured, mix in the mushrooms and onions, then sprinkle in the paprika and cayenne along with a good pinch of salt and pepper.

Reduce the heat to low and stir in the crème fraiche. Let the crème fraiche melt in, then bring to a gentle simmer and stir in the dijon and baby spinach.

Taste for seasoning, then squeeze in the lemon juice and serve up with the green beans.

Sweet Treats

Chocolate mousse

* Makes 4
* Longer recipe
* Make ahead

200g dark chocolate
4 eggs
1 large scoop (45g) vanilla
protein powder

Break the chocolate into a bowl. Fill a small pan of water about a quarter of the way up. Make sure to pick a pan that the bowl of chocolate fits snugly onto. Put the water on to heat, and when it boils, nestle the bowl on the pan, reduce the heat and leave the chocolate to melt – it should take 6–8 minutes. When melted, turn off the heat and leave while you carry on with the rest of the recipe.

Separate the eggs into two large bowls.

Add the protein powder and about 50ml water to the egg yolks and whisk until the mix becomes a smooth, thick liquid – the consistency of very thick double cream.

Using a clean whisk, whisk up the egg whites until they have ballooned in volume and hold their own weight.

Beat the slightly cooled, melted chocolate into the egg yolk mixture, then tip a third of the egg whites into the same mix and beat in.

Stir the remaining two-thirds of the egg whites through the chocolate mix using a folding, slicing motion.

When all of the whites are well incorporated, divide the mixture between four small glasses and leave to cool and set. The mousses will be ready after about 2 hours.

Baked maple apples

* Serves 4

3 small or 2 large eating apples, cut in half
70g softened butter
25ml maple syrup
1 tsp vanilla extract
½ tsp ground cinnamon
40g raisins

To serve
3 tbsp crème fraiche
30g walnuts, roughly chopped

Preheat the oven to 190°C (fan 170°C/gas mark 5).

Take each apple half, and using a teaspoon, scoop the seeded core out of the apple half and discard. Line the apple halves up in a small roasting tray and slide into the hot oven. Bake the halves for 10 minutes.

While the apples are baking, beat together the butter, maple syrup, vanilla, cinnamon and raisins.

After 10 minutes, remove the apples from the oven and roughly dot and splodge the butter mixture as evenly as possible over the top before returning the apples to the hot oven. Bake for a further 15 minutes.

Remove the apples from the oven. They should be cooked through. (If you like them very soft, then cook on for longer, but cover them to stop the raisins burning.)

Plate the apples up, drop on a little crème fraiche and sprinkle over the chopped walnuts.

BLACKCURRANT
poached pears

* Serves 4
* Make ahead

4 pears, peeled
250ml Ribena
2 star anise
1 large cinnamon stick
1 vanilla pod, seeds scraped
from the inside and reserved
4 tbsp mascarpone
chopped pecans, to serve

Lay the pears in a saucepan that's just big enough to tightly hold them in one layer. Pour over the Ribena, then add just enough water to cover the pears. Add the star anise, cinnamon and vanilla seeds.

Bring slowly to the boil, then reduce the heat and simmer very gently for about 15 minutes, or until a butter knife pushes through the flesh of the pear. When you're happy the pears are cooked, fish them gently out of the liquid onto a dish, then pour over all but about a third of the liquid.

Put the remaining poaching liquid back onto the heat and bring to the boil. Reduce by a third.

When you're ready to serve, lay the pears in bowls and spoon over some of the reduced liquid. Dollop a spoonful of mascarpone onto each plate and finish with a scattering of chopped pecans.

Coconut macaroons

* Makes 6
* Make ahead

2 eggs, whites only
20g caster sugar
1 large scoop (45g) vanilla
protein powder
100g desiccated coconut
50g dark chocolate, melted

Preheat the oven to 160°C (fan 140°C/gas mark 3), and line a flat baking tray with non-stick baking parchment.

Place the egg whites in a large, clean mixing bowl and whisk with an electric hand whisk until the whites are frothy and hold their own weight. Spoon in the sugar a little at a time while continuing to whisk the whites.

When the sugar has all been incorporated, slowly add the protein powder to the egg mix, continuing to mix as you sprinkle it in.

When all the sugar and protein powder has been incorporated, the whites should be glossy and thick. Fold the coconut into the mix, then, using two spoons, dollop six large mounds onto the lined baking tray.

Slide the tray into the oven and bake for 8 minutes.

Remove the macaroons from the oven and let them cool a little, then drizzle the melted chocolate all over. Eat warm or leave to cool to room temperature.

Mango & mint fools

* Serves 4
* Make ahead

2 ripe mangoes, flesh only (390g)

30g icing sugar

1 scoop (30g) vanilla protein powder

275ml double cream

mint leaves, to serve – optional

Roughly chop up three-quarters of the mango flesh and place in a blender. Roughly dice the rest of the mango and reserve for later.

Add the icing sugar and protein powder to the mango and blitz until smooth. Tip the mango puree into a bowl and fold the remaining diced mango through.

Whisk up the double cream until it just holds its own weight, then gently fold into the mango puree, just rippling the two components rather than completely mixing them together.

Carefully dollop the mixture into four glasses, then place in the fridge to cool down for an hour. Just before serving, garnish with mint leaves.

Mini strawb pavlovas

* Makes 6
* Longer recipe

4 eggs, whites only
200g caster sugar
½ tsp white wine vinegar
1 tsp cornflour
400g strawberries, stalk removed and berry cut into thin slices (pound-coin thickness)
juice of ½ lemon
3 tsp icing sugar
400ml double cream
3 digestive biscuits

Preheat the oven to 180°C (fan 160°C/gas mark 4).

Place the egg whites in a large clean bowl and whisk well until light and fluffy and able to hold their own weight. Add 1 tablespoon of sugar and whisk for about 30 seconds before adding another. Continue this process, ensuring you don't add more than 1 tablespoon of sugar at a time, and giving the mix a good whisk until all the sugar is used up and the egg whites are very stiff and glossy.

Add the white wine vinegar and the cornflour and whisk again. Continue to whisk for a good 2–3 minutes to be sure that all the ingredients are absolutely mixed together.

When you are happy with the mix, dollop six large mounds of meringue onto a flat baking tray lined with non-stick baking parchment. Using the back of a spoon, push the centre of each mound down a little to create a nest shape.

Slide the nests into the oven and immediately reduce the heat to 100°C (fan 80°C/gas mark ¼). Leave the nests to cook like this for 30 minutes, then turn the oven off and leave to cool.

Meanwhile, mix the strawberries and lemon juice in a bowl, then sieve over the icing sugar. Leave to sit until you're ready to eat.

Just before serving, whisk up the double cream until it's just thick enough to hold its own weight.

Carefully sit the mini pavlovas on a serving plate, dollop on some double cream and top with the strawberries. Crumble over the digestive biscuits and serve immediately.

Use a clean mixing bowl to whisk up the eggs and sugar and don't rush when spooning in the sugar.

Watermelon jelly

* Serves 6
* Longer recipe
* Make ahead

1 medium watermelon, flesh
only (780g)
200g strawberries, stalks
removed and strawberries
cut roughly, plus extra to
decorate
15 sheets of gelatine
120g sugar

The day before you wish to serve, place the watermelon flesh and chopped strawberries into a food processor and blitz until smooth. Pass the blitzed mix through a sieve, discarding the bits of flesh left behind in the sieve as you go. You should end up with about 1.2 litres of fruit juice.

Submerge the gelatine leaves in cold water and leave to soak for about 5 minutes, or until softened.

Pour about one third of the watermelon and strawberry juice into a saucepan and add the sugar. Turn the heat on under the pan and heat gently, stirring to allow the sugar to dissolve.

Do not let the juice boil, but bring it up to a simmer, then turn off the heat.

Pick out some of the soaked gelatine leaves and give them a good squeeze. Gently lower the leaves into the warm liquid, stirring as they go in. The gelatine will dissolve in the warm liquid. Repeat the process with the remaining leaves.

When all the gelatine has been incorporated into the liquid, stir it back into the main batch of watermelon and strawberry juice. Pour the mix into a large jelly mould, then place in the fridge overnight.

When you're ready to eat, gently warm the jelly mould in warm water, then place a plate on top and flip the whole lot over. The jelly should drop neatly from the mould.

Index

Thank yous

I can't believe I'm writing the acknowledgements for my 6th book already. I want to start by saying a big thank you to my publisher Carole from Bluebird for continuing to help me create beautiful books that I'm really proud of. I've had the same awesome team work on all of my books and I'm really lucky to have Maja and Bianca helping to bring my recipes to life. I absolutely love the photography in this book and I hope you enjoy it too.

Thank you to all of my team including Bev, Megan, Martha and Hockley for all your help and support with this book.

To the Love of my life Rosie. Thank you for bringing me so much happiness and for carrying our first baby into the world this year.

Big up all my besties Nikki, Oscar, George, Luca, Ted, Keads, Justin, Brendon, Gilbert, Seymour, Jonny Martin, and Kleatus. I can't wait to make more memories together.

Finally thank you to everyone who follows me on social media, cooks my recipes and does my workouts. You are my inspiration to keep working hard.

Love, Joe

Want to see more recipes and transform your body? Check out my other life-changing books …

First published 2018 by Bluebird
an imprint of Pan Macmillan
20 New Wharf Road, London N1 9RR
Associated companies throughout the world
www.panmacmillan.com

ISBN 978-1-5098-3609-3

9 8 7 6 5 4 3 2 1

A CIP catalogue record for this book is available from the British Library.

Printed and bound in China.

Publisher **Carole Tonkinson**
Senior Editor **Martha Burley**
Assistant Editor **Hockley Raven Spare**
Senior Production Controller **Ena Matagic**
Art Direction & Design **Jilly Topping**
Prop Styling **Lydia Brun**
Food Styling **Bianca Nice, Sunil Vijayakar, Lizzie Harris**

With thanks to Labour and Wait for loaning products for the
photography. Visit the website at www.labourandwait.co.uk

Visit **www.panmacmillan.com** to read more about all our books and
to buy them. You will also find features, author interviews and news of
any author events, and you can sign up for e-newsletters so that you're
always first to hear about our new releases.